The Lighten Up Cookbook

D1193304

Also in This Series

Homemade Soup Recipes:
103 Easy Recipes for Soups, Stews, Chilis, and Chowders Everyone Will Love

Easy Chicken Recipes:
103 Inventive Soups, Salads, Casseroles, and Dinners Everyone Will Love

Retro Recipes from the '50s and '60s:
103 Vintage Appetizers, Dinners, and Drinks Everyone Will Love

Essential Slow Cooker Recipes:
103 Fuss-Free Slow Cooker Meals Everyone Will Love

Easy Cookie Recipes:
103 Best Recipes for Chocolate Chip Cookies, Cake-Mix Creations, Bars,
and Holiday Treats Everyone Will Love

Everyday Dinner Ideas:
103 Easy Recipes for Chicken, Pasta, and Other Dishes Everyone Will Love

No-Bake Desserts:
103 Easy Recipes for No-Bake Cookies, Bars, and Treats

Family Favorite Casserole Recipes:
103 Comforting Breakfast Casseroles, Dinner Ideas, and Desserts Everyone Will Love

The Lighten Up Cookbook

*103 Easy, Slimmed-Down Favorites
for Breakfast, Lunch, and Dinner
Everyone Will Love*

Addie Gundry

St. Martin's Griffin ✦ New York

Any product brand names listed as recipe ingredients or referred to in recipe titles
are trademarks of their respective brand owners. This is an independent
work not endorsed, sponsored, or authorized by those brand owners.

THE LIGHTEN UP COOKBOOK. Text and photos copyright © 2018 by
Prime Publishing, LLC. All rights reserved. Printed in the United States of America.
For information, address St. Martin's Press, 175 Fifth Avenue, New York, N.Y. 10010.

www.stmartins.com

Photography by Megan Von Schönhoff and Tom Krawczyk

The Library of Congress Cataloging-in-Publication Data is available upon request.

ISBN 978-1-250-16030-0 (trade paperback)
ISBN 978-1-250-16031-7 (ebook)

Our books may be purchased in bulk for promotional, educational, or business
use. Please contact your local bookseller or the Macmillan Corporate and
Premium Sales Department at 1-800-221-7945, extension 5442, or by email at
MacmillanSpecialMarkets@macmillan.com.

First Edition: May 2018

10 9 8 7 6 5 4 3 2 1

393000006053879

To Sarah, my sister (in-law).

Thank you for becoming my sister.

For your continuous love, your sense of humor,

and your kindness. You light up our lives.

Contents

6
Sides

7
Dessert

Introduction

The word "healthy" is a tricky one. The definition is as broad and as personal as a word gets. What's healthy for you may be the opposite for me, and when I think of "healthy" cooking, I unfortunately often think of less flavor and less fun. So instead of focusing on that word, "healthy," a word that means so many things, I have decided to take on a different challenge: take 103 beloved recipes and make them a little "lighter."

We've all had moments where we feel like we overindulged, or it's the week leading up to a big event and we want to lay off the salt and consume as many greens as possible. I can't begin to count these moments on my hands because there are far too many. In the past, I have compromised quality and variety and turned to boring food items or prepackaged protein bars. One day, I decided that something lighter can (and should!) pack a punch. Flavor and excitement do not need to fall to the wayside when creating a guilt-free dish.

For me, "lightening up" means using fresh ingredients when I can, instead of something artificial. It means loading up my grocery cart with more items from the produce section than I usually would. It means using ingredients that I can pronounce, and that aren't loaded up with preservatives and additives. And while you can't always achieve perfection, striving toward a healthier lifestyle is a process, one that I hope this book can help you apply to all of your cooking endeavors.

Do you love those cheesy nachos you make and eat when watching the big game? Try my Skinny Bell Pepper Nacho Boats (page 69). Hard to pass up grilled shrimp on the menu? Make my skinny version (page 78). Thinking creamy pasta is removed from the list? Think again! Creamy Avocado Spinach Pasta (page 151) is just as silky and comforting. And don't worry; we can still eat dessert! My favorite is the Clean-Eating Carrot Cake (page 217). It's so good you won't know you're eating light! And go ahead—try it for breakfast!

This book is a collection of 103 favorite recipes that, with simple tweaks and twists, we can change up and make lighter, while maintaining the classic flavor and feeling. Why 103? When you come to our house, we want you to know you can always bring a friend, or two, or three. One hundred felt so rigid, and when creating recipes and sharing them with friends and family, there is always room for three more.

—Addie Gundry

1

Breakfast and Smoothies

When I start my day off by eating something healthy, I feel motivated to keep eating lighter recipes all day long. I'm not going to have a delicious Nutrient-Rich Kale Smoothie (page 20) and then follow that up with a lunch of a burger and fries. It just doesn't make sense! From Banana Nut Bread (page 4) to Breakfast Stuffed Peppers (page 16) and everything in between, there are plenty of ways to make sure you start your day off right.

Banana Nut Bread

Yield: Serves 12 | Prep Time: 10 minutes | Cook Time: 45–55 minutes

Applesauce is such an easy alternative to use when you're looking to lighten up a recipe. It's often used to replace oil in baking. It's just as yummy but cuts back on fat and calories (with no added sugar)! And as a bonus, the almond flour makes this recipe gluten-free!

INGREDIENTS

2 ripe bananas

3 large eggs, room temperature

½ cup applesauce

2 tablespoons vegetable or canola oil

2¼ cups almond flour

1 tablespoon baking powder

1 teaspoon cinnamon

½ teaspoon kosher salt

½ cup chopped pecans

1 teaspoon vanilla extract

DIRECTIONS

1. Preheat the oven to 350°F. Coat a 9 × 5-inch loaf pan with cooking spray. Line the bottom of the pan with parchment paper and coat with cooking spray again.

2. Mash the bananas and place into a 2-cup liquid measuring cup.

3. Add the eggs, applesauce, and vegetable oil to the bananas. Stir to blend. Add enough water to fill the measuring cup of wet ingredients to 2 cups.

4. In a medium bowl, combine the flour, baking powder, cinnamon, and salt.

5. Add the wet ingredients to the dry ingredients and mix just until combined. Do not overmix.

6. Stir in the pecans and vanilla.

7. Pour the batter into the prepared loaf pan and bake for 45 to 55 minutes until golden.

8. Place the bread, in the pan, on a wire rack to cool for 15 minutes.

9. Run a knife or flat metal spatula around the pan. Carefully turn the bread out of the pan onto the rack to cool further. Slice and serve.

Make-Ahead Breakfast Casserole

Yield: Serves 10–12 | Prep Time: 20 minutes | Cook Time: 50–55 minutes

Turkey is a leaner meat than beef, so if you're ever looking to make your favorite beef recipe a little lighter, try it with turkey! It'll fill you up just the same without sacrificing taste.

INGREDIENTS

1 pound turkey breakfast sausage links

1 red bell pepper, cut into 1-inch dice

1 small onion, finely diced

1 (8-ounce) package white button mushrooms, sliced

1 cup spinach

4 zucchini, thinly sliced

½ teaspoon kosher salt

½ teaspoon freshly ground black pepper

¼ teaspoon garlic powder

¼ teaspoon red pepper flakes

1 teaspoon hot sauce

1½ cups cottage cheese

1 cup shredded reduced-fat sharp cheddar cheese

1 cup shredded reduced-fat Parmesan cheese

6 large eggs, lightly beaten

DIRECTIONS

1. Preheat the oven to 350°F. Lightly coat a 9 × 13-inch baking dish with cooking spray.

2. In a large skillet, add the sausage and sauté until fully cooked, about 5 minutes. Break up into pieces and continue to cook until browned.

3. Remove from the pan with a slotted spoon and place on a plate lined with paper towels.

4. Add the bell pepper and onion to the same skillet and sauté until tender, about 4 minutes.

5. Add the mushrooms and cook for about 4 minutes. Add the spinach, mix, and turn off the heat.

6. In a large bowl, combine the zucchini with the salt, black pepper, garlic powder, red pepper flakes, and hot sauce.

7. Stir in the cottage cheese, cheddar cheese, and Parmesan cheese.

8. Mix in the cooked sausage. Mix in the cooked vegetables, then the eggs.

9. Spoon the mixture into the baking dish. Bake for 40 to 45 minutes until set and the cheese has melted. Allow to cool for 5 to 10 minutes before serving.

NOTES

You can make this casserole the day before and refrigerate it to bake later. Remove the casserole from the fridge 30 minutes before baking to warm.

Broccoli and Cheddar Quiche with Brown Rice Crust

Yield: Serves 6 | Prep Time: 20 minutes | Cook Time: 50 minutes

This brown rice crust is a healthier departure from the typical buttery flaky pastry. The crust recipe could even be repurposed when making pumpkin pie or savory tarts for a fun new twist.

INGREDIENTS

2 cups cooked brown rice, cooled (see Notes)

1¼ cups finely grated cheddar cheese

¼ cup finely grated Parmesan cheese

5 large eggs

½ teaspoon herbes de Provence

1 pinch nutmeg

Salt and pepper, to taste

2 cups broccoli florets, blanched

6 ounces cremini mushrooms, chopped

4 scallions, sliced

DIRECTIONS

1. Preheat the oven to 450°F.

2. Combine the rice, ¼ cup of the cheddar cheese, the Parmesan cheese, and 1 egg.

3. Press the mixture into the bottom and up the sides of a 9-inch pie pan to ¼-inch thickness.

4. Bake for 7 minutes until the crust begins to brown.

5. In a large bowl, beat the remaining 4 eggs with the herbes de Provence, nutmeg, salt, and pepper.

6. After the crust has baked, lower the oven temperature to 375°F.

7. Layer the broccoli, mushrooms, remaining 1 cup cheddar cheese, and scallions onto the crust.

8. Pour the egg mixture over the vegetables and cheese. Bake for 35 to 40 minutes until set and the top is golden.

NOTES

You'll need about ⅔ cup uncooked brown rice to yield 2 cups cooked.

Southern Johnny Cakes

Yield: Serves 4–6 | Prep Time: 5 minutes | Cook Time: 10–12 minutes

Johnny cakes are an American classic both in the Northeast and in the South. The addition of whole wheat flour helps add fiber, so if you want to indulge in a bit of maple syrup to top them off, go ahead!

INGREDIENTS

½ cup whole wheat flour

1 cup self-rising cornmeal

1 teaspoon baking powder

1 tablespoon sugar

½ teaspoon kosher salt

2 large eggs, lightly beaten

1 cup buttermilk

1 tablespoon unsalted butter, melted

2 teaspoons vanilla extract

Greek yogurt and fresh berries for topping

DIRECTIONS

1. In a large bowl, combine the flour, cornmeal, baking powder, sugar, and salt.

2. Whisk in the eggs, buttermilk, butter, and vanilla.

3. Coat a griddle or skillet with cooking spray and heat over medium-high heat.

4. Drop about ¼ cup of the batter per cake onto the griddle and cook for 2 to 3 minutes per side until golden brown.

5. Serve with Greek yogurt and fresh berries.

Greek Yogurt Breakfast Bark

Yield: Serves 6–8 | Prep Time: 10 minutes plus 2 hours chill time | Cook Time: N/A

When I'm running late to work in the morning, I often just grab the nearest muffin or waffle and head out the door. Breakfast bark allows me to keep nibbling away at something as I try to find my purse and shoes, while still feeling good knowing that it's full of good-for-you ingredients like fruit and nuts!

INGREDIENTS

1½ cups Greek yogurt

2 tablespoons maple syrup

1 tablespoon honey

½ cup mixed berry granola, such as Quaker Real Medleys Granola

½ cup blueberries

6 strawberries, 3 sliced and 3 chopped

¼ cup pistachios

DIRECTIONS

1. Line a 9 × 13-inch baking pan (or 8 × 8-inch baking pan if you want a thicker bark) with parchment paper, leaving an overhang on two sides.

2. In a small bowl, combine the yogurt, maple syrup, and honey.

3. Pour the mixture into the baking pan and spread it to about ¼ inch to ½ inch thick.

4. Sprinkle the granola, blueberries, strawberries (sliced and chopped), and pistachios over the yogurt mixture.

5. Cover the baking pan with foil and place in the freezer for at least 2 hours.

6. Break or cut into pieces. Put on a platter and serve.

VARIATIONS

Use different granola flavor combinations, fruits, and nuts. You can also add coconut and dark chocolate chips.

Oatmeal Coffee Cake

Yield: Serves 4–6 | Prep Time: 10 minutes | Cook Time: 25–30 minutes

Coffee cake always marked a special occasion growing up. If we were expecting overnight guests, my dad would pick up a coffee cake from the local bakery to serve in the morning alongside some freshly brewed coffee. It was such a fun treat, and with this lightened-up version, I don't have to wait for a special occasion to indulge!

INGREDIENTS

½ cup coconut oil, plus 1 tablespoon

2 large eggs

1¼ cups packed light brown sugar

1 cup cooked oatmeal, cooled

1 teaspoon vanilla extract

¾ cup whole wheat flour

¾ cup all-purpose flour

½ teaspoon kosher salt

1½ teaspoons cinnamon

1 teaspoon baking soda

1½ cups blueberries

¼ cup chopped walnuts

DIRECTIONS

1. Preheat the oven to 350°F. Lightly coat an 8 × 8-inch baking dish with cooking spray.

2. In a large bowl, combine ½ cup of the coconut oil, the eggs, 1 cup of the brown sugar, the oatmeal, and the vanilla.

3. In a medium bowl, whisk together the whole wheat flour, all-purpose flour, salt, 1 teaspoon of the cinnamon, and the baking soda.

4. Combine the dry ingredients with the wet and stir until combined.

5. Gently fold in the blueberries.

6. Pour into the baking dish.

7. In a small bowl, mix together the remaining 1 tablespoon coconut oil, ¼ cup brown sugar, and ½ teaspoon cinnamon with the walnuts. Evenly sprinkle the mixture over the top of the cake.

8. Bake for 25 to 30 minutes until the cake is set.

9. Let the cake cool before cutting. Serve.

Breakfast Stuffed Peppers

Yield: Serves 6 | Prep Time: 15 minutes | Cook Time: 45 minutes

Yes, stuffed peppers are typically made for dinner. But you find bell peppers in omelets and breakfast skillets, so why can't you change the format of the ingredients to make a breakfast version of stuffed peppers? Plus, you get even more veggies than you normally would with each serving.

INGREDIENTS

3 large red or yellow bell peppers (or a combination of colors)

½ pound ground turkey sausage

3 tablespoons olive oil

1–2 red potatoes, peeled and finely diced (1 cup)

1–2 sweet potatoes, peeled and finely diced (1 cup)

½ cup finely minced shallots

1 tablespoon minced garlic

1 tablespoon Italian seasoning

1 tablespoon fresh thyme

½ teaspoon kosher salt

¼ teaspoon freshly ground black pepper

1 tablespoon maple syrup

6 large eggs, whisked together

½ cup shredded low-fat Colby Jack cheese

DIRECTIONS

1. Preheat the oven to 375°F. Lightly coat a baking dish with cooking spray.

2. Slice the peppers in half through the top of the stem. Remove the seeds and interior membrane. Rinse and dry the peppers. Place cut-side up in the baking dish.

3. In a medium skillet, cook the sausage for about 3 minutes, until fully cooked. Remove to a large bowl.

4. Wipe out the skillet, add the olive oil, and warm over medium-high heat.

5. Add the red potatoes, sweet potatoes, and shallots. Then add the garlic, Italian seasoning, thyme, salt, and black pepper. Cook for 5 minutes.

6. Remove the potato mixture from the heat and add to the bowl with the sausage. Mix in the maple syrup.

7. Fill each pepper three-quarters full with the sausage and potato mixture.

8. Add some of the whisked egg to the top of each of the peppers.

9. Bake for 35 minutes or until the eggs have set.

10. Sprinkle each pepper with the Colby Jack cheese. Serve.

NOTES

If the peppers will not
sit up straight in the
baking dish, place some
crumpled foil between
them to prop them up.

Cranberry Orange Scones

Yield: 8 scones | Prep Time: 15 minutes | Cook Time: 18–21 minutes

Scones are my go-to lazy Sunday morning breakfast food. I love to just sit out on the back deck, book in hand, as I get ready to take on the rest of the day. The use of whole wheat flour and low-fat buttermilk helps make this a lighter version than your typical scone. Feel free to substitute your favorite type of berry for the cranberries!

INGREDIENTS

Scones

1½ cups whole wheat flour

1 tablespoon orange zest

1½ teaspoons baking powder

½ teaspoon kosher salt

4 tablespoons cold unsalted butter, cubed

½ cup low-fat buttermilk

3 tablespoons maple syrup

3 tablespoons orange juice

1 teaspoon vanilla extract

¾ cup dried cranberries

2 teaspoons skim milk

Glaze

¼ cup confectioners' sugar

1–2 tablespoons orange juice

DIRECTIONS

1. *For the scones:* Preheat the oven to 425°F. Line a baking sheet with parchment paper.

2. In a medium bowl, combine the flour, orange zest, baking powder, and salt.

3. Cut in the cold butter with a pastry cutter until the mixture forms fine clumps.

4. Gently stir in the buttermilk, maple syrup, orange juice, and vanilla. Fold in the cranberries.

5. Scoop the dough onto the baking sheet and shape the dough in a circle about ¾ inch thick. Brush the top with the milk. Slice the dough into 8 wedges.

6. Bake for 18 to 21 minutes until the scones are golden and are cooked through.

7. Let the scones cool on the baking sheet for 5 minutes, then transfer to a wire rack to cool further.

8. *For the glaze:* Mix the confectioners' sugar and orange juice until it reaches a smooth consistency. Drizzle over the cooled scones.

VARIATIONS

Use fresh cranberries instead of dried.

Nutrient-Rich Kale Smoothie

Yield: Serves 2 | Prep Time: 5 minutes | Cook Time: N/A

Kale is one of those superfoods you always hear so much about. The trick is figuring out how to incorporate it into your meals. I love this smoothie recipe since you can barely even taste the kale with all the yummy fruits inside.

INGREDIENTS

2 cups fresh or frozen kale

½ large banana, sliced and frozen

½ cup frozen blueberries or mixed berries

½ cup frozen pineapple chunks

1 cup filtered water

⅔ cup 100 percent pomegranate juice

Juice of ½ lime

DIRECTIONS

1. Place the kale, banana, blueberries, pineapple chunks, filtered water, pomegranate juice, and lime juice in a blender.

2. Blend until smooth. Pour into glasses and serve.

Cinnamon Roll Smoothie

Yield: Serves 2 | Prep Time: 5 minutes | Cook Time: N/A

When I'm looking to eat healthier, I'll sometimes catch myself daydreaming about all the foods I shouldn't eat: fast-food fries, triple-layer chocolate cake, cheesy lasagna. Cinnamon rolls often enter my thoughts, too, which is why I can't resist this smoothie recipe. I get to satisfy my cravings without all of those extra calories.

INGREDIENTS

1 frozen banana (if using a fresh banana, add 3–4 ice cubes)

½ cup vanilla Greek yogurt

¼ cup old-fashioned oats

¼ cup chopped pecans

1 cup vanilla almond milk

1 tablespoon light brown sugar

½ teaspoon vanilla extract

½ teaspoon cinnamon

DIRECTIONS

1. Place the banana, yogurt, oats, pecans, almond milk, brown sugar, vanilla, and cinnamon in the blender.

2. Blend until smooth. Pour into glasses and serve.

Four-Berry Kiwi Smoothie

Yield: Serves 1 | Prep Time: 10 minutes | Cook Time: N/A

I like to call this my "feeling blue" smoothie. If I'm ever feeling a little down and need to regain that pep in my step, I think of the cheeriest, most concentrated form of energy. I gather all of my favorite fruits in one place, blend them up, and enjoy! Between the kiwi and the lime juice and the mixed berries, there's plenty to smile about.

INGREDIENTS

2¼ cups frozen mixed berries (strawberries, raspberries, blueberries, and blackberries), plus extra for garnish

2 kiwi, peeled and sliced, plus extra for garnish

1 cup orange juice (freshly squeezed, if possible)

1 tablespoon honey (optional)

1 teaspoon lime juice

DIRECTIONS

1. Place the frozen berries in a blender and let thaw for 10 minutes.

2. Add the kiwi, orange juice, honey (if using), and lime juice.

3. Blend on high until smooth.

4. Pour into a glass and garnish with additional kiwi and berries.

2

Soups, Salads, and Sandwiches

After I resolve to start eating healthier, usually after the holidays or as I'm getting ready to enjoy my favorite summer activities, my first step is to ease into bringing homemade lunches to work every day. Once I start bringing along homemade Slow Cooker Vegetable Soup (page 33) or Apple Brie Salad (page 45), I'm able to set my mind to eating healthier in other areas of my life, too.

Low-Calorie Cabbage Soup

Yield: Serves 6 | Prep Time: 15 minutes | Cook Time: 30 minutes

Cabbage doesn't get the attention it deserves. Not only is it filling enough to use in place of a protein, but it's also a wonderful source of nutrition. It's chock-full of vitamins K, C, and B_6, among others. This recipe contains a slew of other veggies, too, so you can enjoy a new flavor in each bite!

INGREDIENTS

1 tablespoon olive oil

1 onion, chopped

2 carrots, chopped

1 zucchini, chopped

3 cloves garlic, minced

4 cups shredded green cabbage

1 cup fire-roasted diced tomatoes

3½ cups low-sodium chicken broth

1 tablespoon tomato paste

1 tablespoon chopped fresh basil

1 tablespoon chopped fresh dill, plus extra for garnish

1 teaspoon dried oregano

¼ teaspoon red pepper flakes

1 bay leaf

½ cup chopped fresh parsley

Salt and black pepper (optional)

1 teaspoon balsamic vinegar

DIRECTIONS

1. Heat the olive oil in a large pot over medium heat. Add the onion and sauté for 2 to 3 minutes or until softened.

2. Add the carrots, zucchini, and garlic and cook for 2 to 3 minutes or until fragrant and softened.

3. Add the cabbage, tomatoes, chicken broth, tomato paste, basil, dill, oregano, red pepper flakes, and bay leaf.

4. Bring to a boil. Lower to a simmer and cook for 25 minutes.

5. Remove the bay leaf. Stir in the parsley. Add salt and black pepper if needed. Stir in the balsamic vinegar.

6. Garnish with additional fresh dill. Ladle into bowls and serve.

Chicken Cannellini Soup

Yield: Serves 6 | Prep Time: 15 minutes | Cook Time: 25 minutes

White beans have certainly made a home in my kitchen. They're loaded up with plenty of fiber, which helps you digest sugar at a slower rate, keeping your glucose levels from rising too fast. I love how this soup contrasts different ingredient textures by incorporating both the soft white beans and the flaky pieces of chicken.

INGREDIENTS

2 tablespoons olive oil

1 onion, roughly chopped

1 carrot, sliced

1 zucchini, sliced

1 red bell pepper, julienned

1 yellow bell pepper, julienned

4 skinless boneless chicken breasts, cooked and cut into small pieces

1 (16-ounce) can navy beans

1 (15.5-ounce) can white cannellini beans

1 (14.5-ounce) can diced tomatoes

4 cups chicken stock

½ tablespoon red paprika

½ tablespoon garlic powder

½ teaspoon cayenne pepper

Salt and pepper to taste

DIRECTIONS

1. In a large pot, heat the olive oil over medium heat. Add the onion and cook, stirring occasionally, until the onion is translucent, 2 to 4 minutes. Add the carrot and cook until the vegetables start to caramelize, about 4 minutes.

2. Add the zucchini and bell peppers. Stir and sauté the vegetables until they start to soften, 2 to 3 minutes.

3. Add the chicken, navy beans, cannellini beans, diced tomatoes, chicken stock, paprika, garlic powder, cayenne pepper, and salt and pepper. Bring to a boil. Cover and cook for 8 minutes.

4. Serve hot.

NOTES

To cook the chicken, place the breasts on a baking sheet and bake at 350°F for 30 minutes.

Slow Cooker Vegetable Soup

Yield: Serves 8 | Prep Time: 15 minutes | Cook Time: 7 hours on Low or 4 hours on High

Any day I can raid the produce aisles of my local grocery store is a day I can feel good about. For me, the more veggies I can use, the better the dish will taste. The variety keeps it exciting up through the very last spoonful! Feel free to substitute the veggies here for others that better suit your tastes.

INGREDIENTS

2 cups frozen corn

2 cups fresh green beans, cut into ¼-inch pieces

2 potatoes, peeled and cut into bite-size cubes

2 carrots, sliced

2–3 stalks celery, diced (1 cup)

1 zucchini, diced

1 small onion, diced

2 (14-ounce) cans fire-roasted diced tomatoes

2 cloves garlic, minced

4 cups low-sodium chicken broth

1 tablespoon Worcestershire sauce

2 teaspoons finely minced thyme

½ teaspoon kosher salt

½ teaspoon freshly ground black pepper

2 bay leaves

DIRECTIONS

1. Lightly spray a 6-quart slow cooker insert with cooking spray.

2. Add the corn, green beans, potatoes, carrots, celery, zucchini, onion, tomatoes, garlic, broth, Worcestershire sauce, thyme, salt, pepper, and bay leaves. Mix well.

3. Cover and cook for 7 hours on Low or 4 hours on High until the vegetables are tender.

4. Remove the bay leaves. Taste and add more salt and pepper if needed. Ladle into bowls and serve.

Lightened-Up Hamburger Soup

Yield: Serves 6 | Prep Time: 15 minutes | Cook Time: 55–60 minutes

It's incredible how a few simple substitutions can make a world of difference in lightening up your favorite recipes. For this hamburger soup, I used a leaner ground beef and low-sodium, fat-free broth, along with plenty of veggies, to make this a guilt-free dish.

INGREDIENTS

1 pound lean ground beef

½ cup chopped onion

2 cloves garlic, minced

2 potatoes, peeled and cut into bite-size pieces

2 carrots, sliced

1 cup fresh green beans, cut into ¼- to ½-inch pieces

½ cup sliced celery

1 (14-ounce) can fire-roasted diced tomatoes

2 tablespoons tomato paste

1 tablespoon Worcestershire sauce

3 cups low-sodium fat-free beef broth

½ teaspoon kosher salt, plus more if needed

¼ teaspoon freshly ground black pepper, plus more if needed

DIRECTIONS

1. In a large soup pot, cook the ground beef, onion, and garlic over medium heat until the beef is browned, about 8 minutes.

2. Add the potatoes, carrots, green beans, and celery. Stir and cook for 7 to 8 minutes or until slightly softened.

3. Add the tomatoes, tomato paste, Worcestershire sauce, beef broth, salt, and pepper. Stir.

4. Bring to a boil, then lower the heat to a simmer and cook for 35 to 40 minutes or until the vegetables are tender.

5. Taste for seasoning and add more salt and pepper if needed.

Tomato-Basil Soup

Yield: Serves 6–8 | Prep Time: 15 minutes | Cook Time: 40–45 minutes

Tomato soup brings me back to my childhood. Whenever I'd go back to school after having stayed home sick, my mom would send me with a thermos of homemade tomato soup, and like magic, it would get me through the day. While I can't legally claim this will cure any ailments, I do think it has a magic all its own.

INGREDIENTS

3 tablespoons olive oil

3 large carrots, diced

1 onion, chopped

2 cloves garlic, minced

¼ cup fresh basil, chopped, or 1 tablespoon dried basil, crushed

3 (28-ounce) cans whole peeled Roma tomatoes

1 quart low-sodium chicken broth

¼ teaspoon red pepper flakes

½ cup fresh parsley, finely chopped

1 tablespoon balsamic vinegar

Salt and pepper to taste

Grilled or toasted bread, for serving

DIRECTIONS

1. In a large pot, heat the olive oil over medium-high heat. Add the carrots, onion, and garlic. Cook for 10 minutes or until the vegetables begin to soften.

2. Add the basil and cook for an additional 5 minutes.

3. Add the tomatoes, chicken broth, and red pepper flakes and bring to a boil.

4. Reduce the heat to a simmer and cook for an additional 25 to 30 minutes.

5. Stir in the parsley, balsamic vinegar, salt, and pepper.

6. Allow the soup to cool slightly.

7. Purée in a blender in batches until smooth.

8. Ladle into bowls and serve with grilled or toasted bread.

Mayo-Free Chicken Salad

Yield: Serves 4 | Prep Time: 15 minutes | Cook Time: N/A

Deli salads are some of the sneakiest foods. You think they must be healthy for you because they have "salad" in the title, but you conveniently forget to take all the mayonnaise into account. For this recipe, I've substituted Greek yogurt for the mayo, and you can't even tell the difference (except maybe in your waistline!).

INGREDIENTS

2 boneless skinless chicken breasts, cooked and cut into bite-size pieces

1 cup diced celery

½ cup finely diced red onion

½ cup cherry tomatoes, cut in half

½ cup plain Greek yogurt

1 avocado, mashed

2 tablespoons chopped fresh cilantro

1 tablespoon olive oil

1 teaspoon lime juice

1 teaspoon garlic powder

½ teaspoon cumin

½ teaspoon kosher salt

¼ teaspoon smoked paprika

4 red or yellow bell peppers, tops cut off and insides scooped and cleaned out

Fresh parsley, for garnish

DIRECTIONS

1. In a large bowl, combine the chicken, celery, onion, and tomatoes.

2. In a small bowl, mix together the yogurt, avocado, cilantro, olive oil, lime juice, garlic powder, cumin, salt, and paprika.

3. Combine the dressing with the chicken mixture.

4. Scoop one-quarter of the chicken salad mixture into each bell pepper. Top with parsley. Serve.

NOTES

To cook the chicken, place the breasts on a baking sheet and bake at 350°F for 30 minutes.

Chicken and Avocado Caesar Salad

Yield: Serves 2 | Prep Time: 20 minutes | Cook Time: 10–12 minutes

By adding chicken and avocado, I finally turned a Caesar salad into a protein-packed stand-alone meal, so I can cut out the afternoon snack! The lower-fat version of Caesar dressing is a great trick, and the Parmesan cheese still makes it feel plenty indulgent.

INGREDIENTS

½ loaf ciabatta bread, sliced

1 tablespoon olive oil, plus 1 teaspoon

Salt and pepper

1 pound boneless skinless chicken breasts

1 cup reduced-fat mayonnaise

2 cloves garlic, minced

3 tablespoons grated Parmesan cheese

2 tablespoons lemon juice

2 teaspoons anchovy paste

1 teaspoon Dijon mustard

8 ounces baby spinach

8 slices reduced-sodium bacon, cooked crisp and crumbled

2 hard-boiled eggs, cut in half

1 avocado, sliced

½ cup shaved Parmesan cheese

DIRECTIONS

1. Preheat the oven to 400°F. Line a baking sheet with parchment paper. Place the ciabatta slices on the baking sheet and drizzle with 1 tablespoon of the olive oil.

2. Bake for 4 to 5 minutes, then flip the slices over and bake until the bread is crispy. Cut the slices in half.

3. Salt and pepper both sides of each chicken breast.

4. In a large nonstick skillet, warm the remaining 1 teaspoon olive oil over medium heat.

5. Add the chicken and sear for 5 to 6 minutes on each side or until fully cooked. Remove to a cutting board, cover with foil, and let rest while you prepare the dressing.

6. In a medium bowl, whisk together the mayonnaise, garlic, grated Parmesan cheese, lemon juice, anchovy paste, mustard, and salt and pepper to taste. Set aside.

7. Slice the chicken.

8. On a large platter or in individual salad bowls, place the spinach, followed by the chicken, bacon, eggs, avocado, shaved Parmesan cheese, and bread slices.

9. Drizzle the dressing over the top. Serve.

Baking Dish Layered Salad

Yield: Serves 10 | Prep Time: 15 minutes | Cook Time: N/A

The hardest part about planning a party is making sure you're offering food that anyone can eat, regardless of their dietary restrictions. This layered salad satisfies everyone from the vegetarians (if you skip the bacon) to the gluten-free folks. Plus, if there's any left over, I can serve it as a side dish for dinner.

INGREDIENTS

8 ounces fresh baby spinach

1 yellow bell pepper, chopped

2 stalks celery, chopped

1 cup cherry tomatoes, cut in half

1 cup frozen peas, thawed

⅓ cup finely chopped red onion

1 cup shredded Colby Jack cheese

6 slices low-sodium bacon, cooked crisp and crumbled (optional)

1 cup reduced-fat buttermilk ranch dressing

DIRECTIONS

1. In a 9 × 13-inch baking dish, layer half of the spinach, bell pepper, celery, tomatoes, peas, onion, Colby Jack cheese, bacon (if using), and buttermilk ranch dressing.

2. Repeat the layers.

3. Serve immediately or chill.

Apple Brie Salad

Yield: Serves 2 | Prep Time: 10 minutes | Cook Time: N/A

The textures offered up in this salad make it a real delight, from the juicy, crunchy apple chunks to the soft cubes of Brie. Plus, this salad uses spinach leaves instead of lettuce, which not only gives it a refreshing taste but also packs it full of nutrients!

INGREDIENTS

6 ounces baby spinach

4 ounces Brie cheese, cut into 1-inch cubes

½ Fuji apple, cored and cut into 1-inch chunks

½ Granny Smith apple, cored and cut into 1-inch chunks

½ cup dried cherries

½ cup walnuts

⅓ cup olive oil

⅓ cup apple cider vinegar

1½ tablespoons honey

1 teaspoon Dijon mustard

¼ teaspoon kosher salt

¼ teaspoon freshly ground black pepper

DIRECTIONS

1. In a large bowl, layer the spinach, cheese, apples, dried cherries, and walnuts.

2. In a small bowl, whisk together the oil, vinegar, honey, mustard, salt, and pepper.

3. Drizzle the dressing over the salad. Serve.

Grandma's Favorite Egg Salad Sandwich

Yield: Serves 4 | Prep Time: 5 minutes | Cook Time: N/A

My grandma and her friends used to meet every Tuesday afternoon to play bridge at the town banquet hall. They'd trade stories and recipes while indulging in the all-you-can-eat buffet. I tagged along one time to try to learn how to play (newsflash: I was terrible), and my grandma kept raving about how I had to try the egg salad because the hint of lemon knocked it out of the park. This version I made recently seems pretty close to Grandma's favorite but with fewer calories.

INGREDIENTS

6 hard-boiled eggs, peeled and chopped

2 tablespoons minced red onion

½ stalk celery, finely chopped

¼ cup reduced-fat mayonnaise

1 tablespoon chopped fresh dill

½ teaspoon dry mustard

2 teaspoons lemon juice

¼ teaspoon kosher salt

¼ teaspoon freshly ground black pepper

8 slices hearty bread

Lettuce leaves

Pickles, for serving

DIRECTIONS

1. In a medium bowl, combine the eggs, onion, celery, mayonnaise, dill, mustard, lemon juice, salt, and pepper.

2. Divide the egg salad onto bread slices with lettuce and a second slice of bread to make 4 sandwiches. Serve with pickles on the side.

Greek Yogurt Chicken Salad Sandwich

Yield: Serves 4 | Prep Time: 15 minutes | Cook Time: N/A

My husband and I like to explore different forest preserves in our area. I pack us lunches, and he acts as the navigator through these unknown paths. Chicken salad sandwiches are his favorite, so I make sure I include a couple for the both of us. And since this chicken salad is mayo-free, he doesn't feel guilty about chowing down on leftovers when we arrive back home.

INGREDIENTS

2 boneless skinless chicken breasts, cooked and cubed

½ cup chopped celery

½ cup diced red onion

½ cup red or green grapes, halved

¼ cup chopped dried cherries

¼ cup chopped walnuts

½ cup plain Greek yogurt

1 tablespoon lemon juice

½ teaspoon garlic powder

Salt and pepper to taste

1 loaf ciabatta bread cut into 4 sandwich-size rolls, split open

4 leaves Boston lettuce

DIRECTIONS

1. In a large bowl, mix together the chicken, celery, onion, grapes, dried cherries, walnuts, yogurt, lemon juice, garlic powder, salt, and pepper.

2. Divide the chicken salad on the ciabatta rolls over a lettuce leaf. Serve.

NOTES

To cook the chicken, place the breasts on a baking sheet and bake at 350°F for 30 minutes.

Chickpea, Avocado, and Pesto Sandwich

Yield: Serves 4 | Prep Time: 10 minutes | Cook Time: N/A

One of my close friends is a vegetarian, and whenever I invite her over for lunch, I try to find something new and interesting to prepare for her other than peanut butter and jelly sandwiches or basic salads. I was so pleased when I put together this sandwich because it actually looks like a hearty, meat-filled sandwich even though there isn't any meat! My vegetarian friend gave it two big thumbs up, too.

INGREDIENTS

1 (15-ounce) can chickpeas, rinsed and drained

1 large ripe avocado

Juice of ½ lemon

Salt and pepper, to taste

8 slices hearty bread, such as 12-grain, lightly toasted

2 tablespoons prepared basil pesto

Baby spinach leaves

2 tomatoes, cut into thick slices

DIRECTIONS

1. In a medium bowl, combine the chickpeas and avocado. Smash with a potato masher until well mixed and at the desired consistency. Stir in the fresh lemon juice. Season with salt and pepper to taste.

2. On each slice of toasted bread, spread the basil pesto. Top 4 slices with the spinach leaves and equal amounts of the chickpea mixture. Place the tomato slices on top. Sprinkle the tomato slices with salt and pepper. Top with the remaining toasted bread slices, cut the sandwiches in half, and serve.

Chicken Caprese Sandwich

Yield: Serves 4 | Prep Time: 10 minutes | Cook Time: 10 minutes

Balsamic vinegar is a much healthier condiment to use on a sandwich than more typical options like ketchup or mayonnaise. The fresh mozzarella and Campari tomatoes are bright and wholesome ingredients that add so much flavor, which is why it's the ideal, elegant dish to serve when you're expecting company.

INGREDIENTS

2 boneless skinless chicken breasts

4 tablespoons extra-virgin olive oil, plus more for drizzling

Kosher salt and freshly ground black pepper

1 loaf sourdough bread, sliced

8 Campari tomatoes

¼ cup fresh basil leaves

8 ounces fresh mozzarella cheese, sliced into rounds

Balsamic vinegar

DIRECTIONS

1. Coat the chicken breasts with 2 tablespoons of the olive oil, salt, and pepper. Allow to sit at room temperature while preparing the grill.

2. Preheat the grill to high. Alternatively, heat a grill pan on the stove over medium-high heat.

3. Add the chicken to the grill or pan. Cook for 3 to 4 minutes, and then turn the chicken breasts. Cook for another 4 minutes or until nice grill marks form. Reduce the heat to medium, cover, and cook until the chicken has an internal temperature of 185°F. Remove from the heat and allow to rest.

4. While the chicken is resting, brush the remaining 2 tablespoons olive oil on the bread and grill until lightly browned.

5. Thinly slice the cooked chicken. Slice the tomatoes.

6. Layer half of the bread slices with basil leaves. Add a few slices of mozzarella cheese, 3 to 4 slices of chicken each, and top with tomato slices. Drizzle with olive oil and balsamic vinegar. Top with another slice of bread.

7. Season with salt and pepper and serve.

3

Appetizers

Appetizers are the hidden curse of all my diet attempts. I have enough
willpower to resist unhealthy options for breakfast, lunch, and dinner,
but it's the snacking, whether on my own or with friends, that really trips me
up. If I only provide myself with healthy appetizers, like Parmesan
Cauliflower Bites (page 61) and Turkey Cranberry Meatballs (page 73),
then I don't have to worry about derailing completely.

Skinny Poolside Dip

Yield: Serves 6–8 | Prep Time: 5 minutes | Cook Time: N/A

My neighbors a couple of doors down have a pool, and every Memorial Day they invite a few of the neighbors over for swimming and grilling. They always make a corn and cream cheese dip that I tend to circle back to as I make my rounds. This version is inspired by that Memorial Day dip, but I replaced full-fat cream cheese with a lighter version and added more veggies.

INGREDIENTS

1 (15-ounce) can corn, drained

4 ounces low-fat cream cheese, softened

4 ounces goat cheese, softened

1 red bell pepper, finely diced

1 jalapeño pepper, seeded and finely diced

1 (2.25-ounce) can black olives, finely diced

1 (1-ounce) packet ranch seasoning

1 teaspoon lime zest

1 teaspoon lime juice

Crackers, for serving

DIRECTIONS

1. In a medium bowl, combine the corn, cream cheese, goat cheese, bell pepper, jalapeño, olives, ranch seasoning, lime zest, and lime juice.

2. Serve with crackers.

Zucchini Chips

Yield: Serves 4 | Prep Time: 10 minutes | Cook Time: 20–25 minutes

Some of the best appetizers are crispy, breaded bites. From fried chicken to mozzarella bites to onion rings, there's so much to love. These zucchini chips allow you to enjoy that breaded taste you love with a culinary vegetable, and they're much healthier than popping open a bag of greasy potato chips!

INGREDIENTS

1 cup all-purpose flour

2 large eggs, beaten

1 cup panko bread crumbs

½ cup grated Parmesan cheese

¼ teaspoon dried Italian seasoning

⅛ teaspoon red pepper flakes

2 zucchini, sliced into ¼-inch rounds

Reduced-fat buttermilk ranch dressing, for dipping

DIRECTIONS

1. Preheat the oven to 400°F. Line a baking sheet with parchment paper.

2. Place the flour in a shallow pie plate. Place the eggs in another.

3. In a medium bowl, combine the panko, Parmesan cheese, Italian seasoning, and red pepper flakes.

4. Dip the zucchini rounds into the flour, then the egg.

5. Dip the zucchini into the panko-cheese mixture, pressing the rounds to coat.

6. Place the zucchini rounds on the baking sheet.

7. Bake for 20 to 25 minutes or until golden brown.

8. Serve with ranch dressing.

Parmesan Cauliflower Bites

Yield: 28–32 bites | Prep Time: 15 minutes | Cook Time: 20–25 minutes

Veggies can make some of the yummiest appetizers. When I'm trying to eat healthier, I always make sure to bake any potential veggie dishes so that they're roasted instead of fried. With just a few simple spices, you can turn any veggie into something special.

INGREDIENTS

2 large eggs, beaten

1 cup panko bread crumbs

¾ cup finely grated Parmesan cheese

½ teaspoon Italian seasoning

¼ teaspoon red pepper flakes

½ head cauliflower, cut into bite-size florets

Marinara sauce, for dipping

DIRECTIONS

1. Preheat the oven to 400°F. Line a baking sheet with parchment paper.

2. In a small bowl, place the eggs. In a medium bowl, combine the panko, Parmesan cheese, Italian seasoning, and red pepper flakes.

3. Dip the cauliflower into the beaten eggs, then roll in the panko-cheese mixture to fully coat the florets.

4. Place on the baking sheet. Bake for 20 to 25 minutes or until golden brown.

5. Serve with the marinara sauce.

Southern Deviled Eggs

Yield: Serves 12 | Prep Time: 10 minutes | Cook Time: N/A

Eggs are a great source of protein, so I love finding ways to work them into my menu. By using reduced-fat mayonnaise and low-fat sour cream, I've cut back on some of the calories, so you get all the benefits of enjoying an egg dish without any of the drawbacks.

INGREDIENTS

6 hard-boiled eggs, peeled and cut in half with whites and yolks separated

2 tablespoons reduced-fat mayonnaise

2 tablespoons low-fat sour cream

1 tablespoon sweet pickle relish

1 teaspoon apple cider vinegar

½ teaspoon dry mustard

Smoked paprika, for garnish

Chopped pimentos, for garnish

DIRECTIONS

1. In a small bowl, combine the egg yolks, mayonnaise, sour cream, relish, apple cider vinegar, and mustard and mash until smooth.

2. Fill the egg white halves with the yolk mixture.

3. Sprinkle with paprika and pimentos. Serve.

Easy Cucumber Cups

Yield: Serves 8 | Prep Time: 15 minutes | Cook Time: N/A

One easy way to lighten up a typical crackers-with-tuna-topping dish is to use cucumber rounds instead of crackers! The cucumbers make the whole snack much more refreshing since there's a juicy crunch with each bite.

INGREDIENTS

2 English cucumbers, cut into 1-inch slices

1 (5-ounce) can white Albacore tuna in water, well drained

¼ cup reduced-fat mayonnaise

1 tablespoon capers, drained

1 teaspoon lemon zest

½ teaspoon kosher salt

¼ teaspoon freshly ground black pepper

Fresh dill, for garnish

DIRECTIONS

1. Using a melon baller, scoop a small indentation in each cucumber cup.

2. In a small bowl, combine the tuna, mayonnaise, capers, lemon zest, salt, and pepper.

3. Fill each cucumber cup with the tuna mixture. Top each cup with dill and serve.

Baked Buffalo Chicken Rolls

Yield: 12 rolls | Prep Time: 15 minutes | Cook Time: 12–15 minutes

Buffalo chicken is a staple at sporting events. How could you watch a football game without a beer in hand next to a bucket of buffalo wings? My husband challenged me to find a healthier alternative, and when he tried one of these, he was impressed. The chicken isn't fried, and the rolls themselves are baked, which makes these a much lighter option.

INGREDIENTS

1 boneless skinless chicken breast, cooked and shredded

½ cup buffalo hot sauce

1 cup packaged coleslaw mix

½ cup diced celery

12 egg roll wrappers

1 cup crumbled blue cheese

Blue cheese dressing, for serving

DIRECTIONS

1. Preheat the oven to 400°F. Coat a baking sheet with cooking spray.

2. In a small bowl, combine the chicken with the hot sauce.

3. In another small bowl, mix the coleslaw mix with the diced celery.

4. Place an egg roll wrapper diagonally on a flat surface.

5. Place 1 tablespoon of the coleslaw-celery mixture on the lower bottom of the wrapper. Next place 2 tablespoons of the chicken mixture on top. Spoon 1 tablespoon of the blue cheese on top of the chicken.

6. Carefully fold the bottom corner of the wrapper over the filling. Next fold the right corner over, then the left, forming an envelope. Roll the wrap upward almost to the top. Moisten the top with water, then fold over and seal. Repeat with the remaining wrappers.

7. Place the rolls on the baking sheet. Lightly spray each roll with cooking spray.

8. Bake for 12 to 15 minutes until the rolls are golden brown and crisp.

9. Serve with blue cheese dressing.

NOTES

To cook the chicken, place the breast on a baking sheet and bake at 350°F for 30 minutes.

Skinny Bell Pepper Nacho Boats

Yield: 18 boats | Prep Time: 15 minutes | Cook Time: 10 minutes

Nachos are another sporting staple that needed a healthy makeover. It's the chips that tend to be the most problematic. They break easily and aren't particularly filling, causing you to grab more and more. Using mini bell peppers gives the nachos even more substance while cutting back on unnecessary calories.

INGREDIENTS

1 pound mini bell peppers (about 8 peppers)

2 boneless skinless chicken breasts, cooked and shredded

1 cup salsa

1 teaspoon chili powder

1 teaspoon cumin

¼ teaspoon kosher salt

½ teaspoon freshly ground black pepper

1 cup shredded, reduced-fat Monterey Jack cheese

Chopped fresh cilantro, for garnish

Sour cream, for serving

DIRECTIONS

1. Preheat the oven to 350°F. Line a baking sheet pan with parchment paper.

2. Slice the tops off the peppers, then slice each in half lengthwise. Remove the seeds and membranes. Set on the baking sheet.

3. In a medium bowl, combine the chicken, salsa, chili powder, cumin, salt, and black pepper.

4. Evenly spoon the chicken mixture into each pepper.

5. Top with the Monterey Jack cheese and bake for 10 minutes until the cheese has melted.

6. Top the peppers with cilantro. Serve with sour cream.

NOTES

To cook the chicken, place the breasts on a baking sheet and bake at 350°F for 30 minutes.

Cucumber Avocado Rolls

Yield: 12 rolls | Prep Time: 20 minutes | Cook Time: N/A

By using long slices of cucumber as the "bread," you can cut down on calories without sacrificing on taste! If you've never used a mandoline slicer before, it might be a good idea to get a couple of extra cucumbers to use as practice until you get the hang of it.

INGREDIENTS

2 English cucumbers

½ cup chive cream cheese, softened

1 avocado, diced

2 ounces smoked salmon, cut into bite-size pieces

DIRECTIONS

1. Using a mandoline or a vegetable peeler, thinly slice the cucumbers lengthwise.

2. Set the sliced cucumbers on paper towels to absorb the excess liquid.

3. At one end of each cucumber slice, place a dollop of the cream cheese, then some of the diced avocado and salmon.

4. Gently roll up the cucumber with the filling. Secure the cucumber roll with a toothpick. Serve.

Turkey Cranberry Meatballs

Yield: 28 meatballs | Prep Time: 15 minutes | Cook Time: 15 minutes

I feel like I'm secretly planning my Thanksgiving dinner all year long. I'll randomly dwell on different potato dishes to serve or the sweet taste of cranberries throughout the year. When I start craving a small taste of the holiday season, I love making these Turkey Cranberry Meatballs.

INGREDIENTS

1 cup barbecue sauce

¼ cup orange marmalade

1 egg white

1 (20-ounce) package extra-lean ground turkey

½ cup dried cranberries

3 scallions, finely chopped

1 tablespoon reduced-sodium soy sauce

¼ teaspoon kosher salt

¼ teaspoon freshly ground black pepper

DIRECTIONS

1. In a small bowl, combine the barbecue sauce and marmalade. Set aside.

2. In a medium bowl, whisk the egg white. Add the turkey, cranberries, scallions, soy sauce, salt, and pepper, and mix well until combined.

3. Shape the turkey mixture into 28 golf ball–size meatballs.

4. Spray a large nonstick skillet with cooking spray.

5. Add the meatballs and cook over medium-high heat until fully cooked through and evenly browned.

6. Pour the barbecue sauce mixture over the meatballs and stir to coat. Lower the heat to low.

7. Place a lid over the skillet and cook for 3 minutes.

8. Place a toothpick into each meatball and serve.

Slow Cooker Spinach and Artichoke Dip

Yield: Serves 6–8 | Prep Time: 10 minutes | Cook Time: 3–4 hours on Low or 1½–2 hours on High

Spinach and artichoke dip has an unshakeable hold on me. If someone orders it at a restaurant, I eat much more than my fair share. By using a few lighter ingredients, you can make a dip that's just as addicting.

INGREDIENTS

1 (13.75-ounce) can quartered artichoke hearts, drained and chopped

10 ounces fresh baby spinach, roughly chopped

1 cup shredded Monterey Jack cheese

½ cup grated Parmesan cheese

⅓ cup finely diced red onion

1 (8-ounce) package reduced-fat cream cheese, cut into cubes

½ cup light sour cream

½ cup crème fraîche

½ cup skim milk

4 cloves garlic, finely minced

¼ teaspoon nutmeg

¼ teaspoon kosher salt

½ teaspoon freshly ground black pepper

Pita chips or crackers, for serving

DIRECTIONS

1. Lightly spray the insert of a 6-quart slow cooker with cooking spray.

2. Add the artichoke hearts, spinach, Monterey Jack cheese, Parmesan cheese, onion, cream cheese, sour cream, crème fraîche, milk, garlic, nutmeg, salt, and pepper. Mix until well combined.

3. Cover and cook for 3 to 4 hours on Low or 1½ to 2 hours on High.

4. Serve with pita chips or crackers.

Smoked Salmon and Cream Cheese Bites

Yield: 40 bites | Prep Time: 20–25 minutes | Cook Time: N/A

Salmon provides so many health benefits, so I like to work it into recipes when I can. Eating salmon can improve both your cardiovascular health and your brain function—how great is that? By pairing these with cucumbers, you get something a little bit fancy, a little bit sophisticated, and a whole lot of yum.

INGREDIENTS

3 English cucumbers, peeled and cut into ½-inch slices

1 (8-ounce) package cream cheese, softened

¼ cup crème fraîche

3 tablespoons chopped fresh dill

1 tablespoon horseradish

1 teaspoon lemon zest

½ teaspoon lemon juice

Capers, drained (about ¼ cup)

1 pound smoked salmon, cut into bite-size pieces

Dill fronds, for garnish

DIRECTIONS

1. Using a melon baller, scoop a small depression in the top of each cucumber slice, forming a little cup. Place the slices on a paper towel to dry while preparing the cream cheese topping.

2. In a medium bowl, combine the cream cheese, crème fraîche, chopped dill, horseradish, lemon zest, and lemon juice.

3. Scoop 1 teaspoon of the cream cheese mixture into each cucumber cup. Sprinkle a few capers on top of the cream cheese. Add a piece of smoked salmon and top with a dill frond. Serve.

Grilled Shrimp

Yield: Serves 4–6 | Prep Time: 10 minutes | Cook Time: 5 minutes

Grilled shrimp is a signature appetizer at restaurants such as Bonefish Grill and the Cheesecake Factory. This lightened-up version incorporates Greek yogurt in the dip to keep it light and healthy.

INGREDIENTS

¼ cup plain Greek yogurt

¼ cup sweet chili sauce

½ tablespoon sriracha sauce, or more to taste

3 tablespoons chopped scallions

1 pound shrimp, uncooked, shelled, and deveined

Salt and pepper

1 tablespoon olive oil

Juice of ½ lemon

Lemon wedges, for serving

DIRECTIONS

1. In a small bowl, combine the Greek yogurt, sweet chili sauce, and sriracha sauce. Stir well to combine. Taste and add more sriracha if desired. Pour into a small serving dish and top with the scallions. Set aside.

2. Meanwhile, in a large bowl, mix the shrimp with salt, pepper, olive oil, and lemon juice. Stir to combine and allow to sit at room temperature for 5 minutes.

3. Preheat a grill to high. Alternatively, heat a grill pan on the stovetop over medium-high heat.

4. Add the shrimp to the grill or pan. Cook for about 2 minutes and then turn the shrimp. Cook for another 2 minutes. The shrimp will turn pink and begin to curl. Remove from the heat to a serving platter.

5. Serve with the spicy dipping sauce and lemon wedges.

4

Meat and Poultry

One of the lessons I learned while writing this book was that eating healthier didn't necessarily mean I had to cut out all of the dishes and ingredients that I loved. It just meant I needed to go about the process in a smarter way. Whether I am substituting veggies for noodles in the Zucchini Lasagna (page 111) or making the most out of everyday ingredients in the Easy Baked Lemon Chicken (page 91), just by thinking outside the box, I didn't sacrifice the foods I rely on the most.

Chicken Noodle Casserole with Corn and Zucchini

Yield: Serves 8 | Prep Time: 20 minutes | Cook Time: 30 minutes

When I was in elementary school, a friend's family would invite me over for casserole night. The casserole was the star of the dinner table, and oftentimes there'd be some variation on a chicken and pasta casserole. This version is a little lighter with the use of whole wheat pasta and plenty of veggies, but it'll make casserole night just as memorable.

INGREDIENTS

1 tablespoon unsalted butter

⅔ cup all-purpose flour

3 cups low-sodium chicken broth

1 cup 2% milk

2 teaspoons fresh thyme

1 teaspoon kosher salt

8 ounces regular, whole-wheat, or gluten-free pasta, cooked and drained (I used cavatappi)

2 boneless skinless chicken breasts, cooked and diced

1½ cups shredded reduced-fat mozzarella cheese

1 zucchini, diced into small pieces

1½ cups frozen corn kernels

¼ cup grated Parmesan cheese

DIRECTIONS

1. Preheat the oven to 350°F. Lightly coat a 9 × 13-inch baking dish with cooking spray and set aside.

2. Melt the butter in a large skillet over medium-high heat. Add the flour and stir to cook for about 1 minute. Whisk in the broth until well combined and there are no lumps. Add the milk, thyme, and salt and bring to a simmer, stirring constantly. Allow the sauce to cook until it thickens, whisking frequently, for 5 to 7 minutes.

3. Remove the sauce from the heat and stir in the cooked pasta, chicken, ½ cup of the mozzarella cheese, the zucchini, and the corn.

4. Transfer the mixture to prepared baking dish. Top with the remaining 1 cup mozzarella cheese and sprinkle with the Parmesan cheese.

5. Bake, uncovered, until bubbly and heated through, about 20 minutes. Serve.

NOTES

To cook the chicken, place the breasts on a baking sheet and bake at 350°F for 30 minutes.

Slow Cooker Italian Chicken

Yield: Serves 8 | Prep Time: 10 minutes | Cook Time: 6–8 hours on Low or 3–4 hours on High

There's some debate about whether chicken thighs or chicken breasts are the healthier option when cooking. It really comes down to how you choose to cook them. Since the chicken thighs in this recipe aren't fried up in layers of oil, they're able to maintain their nutritional benefits, making them a fantastic option for dinner.

INGREDIENTS

1 (28-ounce) can whole tomatoes, undrained

1 cup cremini mushrooms, quartered

2 carrots, diced

1 small bell pepper, seeded and large diced

1 small onion, diced

3 cloves garlic, minced

2 tablespoons tomato paste

1 teaspoon dried basil

½ teaspoon dried marjoram

½ teaspoon dried parsley

½ teaspoon dried oregano

½ teaspoon dried rosemary

½ teaspoon red pepper flakes

2 pounds boneless skinless chicken thighs

Cooked regular, whole-wheat, or gluten-free pasta, or rice, for serving

DIRECTIONS

1. Lightly spray the insert of an 8-quart slow cooker with cooking spray. Add the tomatoes with their juices and smash with the back of a wooden spoon.

2. Add the mushrooms, carrots, bell pepper, onion, garlic, tomato paste, basil, marjoram, parsley, oregano, rosemary, and red pepper flakes. Stir to combine.

3. Lay the chicken thighs evenly over the tomato mixture and stir to coat. Cover and cook for 6 to 8 hours on Low or for 3 to 4 hours on High.

4. Shred the chicken before serving.

5. Serve over pasta or rice.

20-Minute Skillet Chicken and Spinach Parmesan

Yield: Serves 4 | Prep Time: 5 minutes | Cook Time: 20 minutes

One of the easiest ways to feel less guilty about a recipe is to incorporate some spinach. You get the opportunity to work in a nutritious superfood while maintaining the same taste you've come to expect. Plus, you don't have to wait hours for this dish to finish baking in the oven—it's done cooking in only 20 minutes!

INGREDIENTS

1 large egg

1 cup panko bread crumbs

¼ cup grated Parmesan cheese

4 boneless skinless chicken breasts

Salt and pepper

4 tablespoons olive oil

1½ cups marinara sauce

2 cups baby spinach

4 ounces fresh mozzarella cheese, cut into 4 slices

DIRECTIONS

1. In a shallow dish, whisk the egg with 2 tablespoons water.

2. Combine the panko and Parmesan cheese in a small bowl.

3. Lightly season the chicken with salt and pepper and place into the dish with the egg mixture. Turn to coat evenly.

4. Coat the chicken with the panko mixture, pressing gently to adhere.

5. Heat 2 tablespoons of the olive oil in a large, oven-safe skillet over medium-high heat.

6. Add 2 chicken pieces to the pan and cook for 3 to 4 minutes on each side until golden brown and cooked through. Wipe the pan clean and repeat with the remaining oil and chicken.

7. Remove the chicken from the skillet and pour half of the pasta sauce into the bottom of the skillet.

8. Place the baby spinach in 4 piles around the pan. Gently lay one piece of chicken on top of each pile.

9. Evenly top each piece of chicken with the remaining sauce and mozzarella slices.

10. Heat under the broiler for 2 to 4 minutes until the cheese just melts and begins to brown.

11. Serve immediately.

Crunchy Chicken Casserole

Yield: Serves 6–8 | Prep Time: 10 minutes | Cook Time: 30 minutes

Casserole toppings have so many variations. My uncle always uses butter crackers, my grandma loves panko bread crumbs, and one of my best friends swears by potato chips. This is another winning variation where I used both cornflakes and almonds to give the dish a sweet crunch (without the unhealthy preservatives in potato chips).

INGREDIENTS

3 boneless skinless chicken breasts, cooked and chopped

1 cup shredded reduced-fat mozzarella cheese

1 cup chopped red bell pepper

¼ cup chopped celery

¼ cup sliced scallions

1 (10¾-ounce) can reduced-fat and reduced-sodium condensed cream of chicken soup

¼ cup 2% milk

Salt and pepper

½ cup cornflakes

¼ cup sliced almonds

DIRECTIONS

1. Preheat the oven to 400°F. Lightly coat an 8 × 8-inch baking dish with cooking spray and set aside.

2. In a large bowl, stir together the chicken, mozzarella cheese, bell pepper, celery, scallions, cream of chicken soup, and milk. Season with salt and pepper to taste. Pour into the casserole dish.

3. Sprinkle the cornflakes and almonds evenly over the chicken mixture.

4. Bake, uncovered, for about 30 minutes or until heated through.

5. Allow to stand for at least 10 minutes before serving.

NOTES

To cook the chicken, place the breasts on a baking sheet and bake at 350°F for 30 minutes.

Easy Baked Lemon Chicken

Yield: Serves 4 | Prep Time: 5 minutes | Cook Time: 20–30 minutes

For many years, I would only make lemon chicken on the stovetop. It was my lazy-day dinner recipe that I could throw together when I didn't feel like cooking. A few months ago when I resolved to eat healthier, I was determined to find a cleaner way to enjoy my lazy-day meal, and this baked version did the trick!

INGREDIENTS

⅓ cup low-sodium chicken broth

¼ cup fresh lemon juice

1 tablespoon honey

2 teaspoons minced garlic

1 teaspoon dried rosemary

1 teaspoon dried basil

1 teaspoon lemon pepper seasoning

Salt and pepper, to taste

3 tablespoons unsalted butter

4 boneless skinless chicken breasts

Lemon slices, for serving (optional)

DIRECTIONS

1. Preheat the oven to 400°F. Line a baking sheet with parchment paper and set aside.

2. In a small bowl, whisk together the broth, lemon juice, honey, garlic, rosemary, basil, lemon pepper seasoning, salt, and pepper.

3. In a large skillet, melt the butter over medium-high heat. Add the chicken and cook for 2 to 3 minutes on each side just until browned but not cooked through. Transfer the chicken to the baking sheet.

4. Pour the prepared sauce over the chicken. Bake for 20 to 30 minutes until the chicken is cooked through. Every 5 to 10 minutes, spoon the sauce from the pan over the chicken.

5. Garnish with lemon slices, if desired, and serve.

Chicken Parmesan Quinoa Bake

Yield: Serves 6 | Prep Time: 10 minutes | Cook Time: 1 hour

The health gurus like to talk about the magic powers of quinoa and how you get so much protein and fiber every time you eat it. It took me a while to jump on the quinoa train, but once I did, I couldn't wait to find new ways to incorporate it into my favorite recipes—like a classic Chicken Parm!

INGREDIENTS

2 tablespoons all-purpose flour

1 cup shredded Parmesan cheese

2 teaspoons garlic powder

1 large egg

6 boneless skinless chicken thighs

1 cup uncooked quinoa

1 green bell pepper, diced

1 cup cremini mushrooms, quartered

½ cup finely diced onion

2 cups jarred marinara sauce

1 cup low-sodium chicken broth

1 tablespoon minced garlic

Salt and pepper, to taste

DIRECTIONS

1. Preheat the oven to 375°F. Lightly coat a 9 × 13-inch casserole dish with cooking spray and set aside.

2. In a medium dish, mix together the flour, Parmesan cheese, and garlic powder.

3. In a shallow bowl, whisk the egg with 2 tablespoons water.

4. Dip the chicken into the egg and then into the Parmesan mixture. Lightly press to generously coat each piece. Set aside.

5. Place the quinoa in the casserole dish and add the bell pepper, mushrooms, and onion. Then add the marinara sauce, broth, and minced garlic to the casserole dish and mix everything together.

6. Place the chicken thighs on top of the quinoa mixture.

7. If there is any remaining Parmesan mixture, evenly sprinkle it over the top of each chicken piece. Season with salt and pepper.

8. Bake, uncovered, for 20 minutes. Then cover with foil and bake for an additional 40 minutes or until the quinoa and chicken are fully cooked. Serve.

One-Pan Roasted Chicken and Veggies

Yield: Serves 2 | Prep Time: 5 minutes | Cook Time: 15 minutes

The healthier alternative to one-pot recipes has to be the underrated one-pan recipe. Roasting is just as simple as throwing everything into a pot on the stovetop. The hardest part about eating healthier is just working more veggies into your diet. Roasting vegetables is one of the easiest ways to get even the most stubborn eater to enjoy them because they're more appealing when they're all warm and crispy.

INGREDIENTS

2 boneless skinless chicken breasts, cubed

1 cup green bell pepper, large diced

1 cup red bell pepper, large diced

1 cup carrot, large diced

1 cup white button mushrooms, quartered

1 cup broccoli florets

½ red onion, coarsely chopped

2 tablespoons olive oil

1 teaspoon Italian seasoning

Salt and pepper, to taste

DIRECTIONS

1. Preheat the oven to 500°F. Line a baking sheet with parchment paper and set aside.

2. Place the chicken, bell peppers, carrots, mushrooms, broccoli, and onion on the baking sheet. Add the olive oil, Italian seasoning, salt, and pepper on top. Toss to combine.

3. Bake for 15 minutes or until the veggies are charred and the chicken is cooked.

4. Serve immediately.

Midnight Breakfast Sausage with Veggies

Yield: Serves 4 | Prep Time: 10 minutes | Cook Time: 15 minutes

Chicken sausage is a healthier alternative to using pork sausage since it's a leaner meat with fewer calories and less fat. Certain stores will even sell it without the pork casing if you're looking to avoid pork altogether.

INGREDIENTS

8 Italian chicken sausages

1 pound baby red potatoes, quartered

1 red onion, chopped

1 red bell pepper, chopped

1 green bell pepper, chopped

4 cloves garlic

2 tablespoons fresh thyme

Salt and pepper

4 teaspoons olive oil

4 large eggs

DIRECTIONS

1. Preheat the oven to 350°F. Line a baking sheet with foil and lightly coat with cooking spray.

2. Add the sausage, potatoes, onion, bell peppers, garlic, and thyme to the baking sheet. Sprinkle generously with salt and pepper. Drizzle with 2 teaspoons of the olive oil. Stir to combine.

3. Place the baking sheet in the oven and bake for 15 to 20 minutes or until the veggies are charred and the sausages are cooked through. Remove from the oven.

4. In a small skillet, heat the remaining 2 teaspoons olive oil over medium-low heat. Fry the eggs until over-easy. Serve over the sausages and veggies.

Spiced Grilled Chicken

Yield: Serves 4 | Prep Time: 5 minutes | Cook Time: 15 minutes

Sauces can sometimes be laden with hidden fat and calories that you wouldn't even think about. It's important to make sure your meals have flavor, but instead of using a rich sauce or dressing, you can often achieve similar results using a variety of spices. Pair this with the Back-to-Basics Broccoli Salad (page 166) or Roasted Parmesan Asparagus (page 170) to complete the meal.

INGREDIENTS

2 tablespoons olive oil

1 teaspoon garlic powder

1 teaspoon cumin

½ teaspoon coriander

½ teaspoon smoked paprika

½ teaspoon chili powder

Kosher salt and freshly ground black pepper, to taste

4 boneless skinless chicken breasts

Prepared coleslaw, for serving

DIRECTIONS

1. Preheat the grill to medium-high heat. Alternatively, heat a grill pan on the stove over medium-high heat.

2. In a small bowl, mix the olive oil, garlic powder, cumin, coriander, paprika, chili powder, salt, and pepper. Mix until combined.

3. Brush the spice mixture over both sides of the chicken.

4. Place the chicken on the grill or pan and grill each side for 4 to 6 minutes until the internal temperature reaches 165°F. Remove from the grill and allow to rest for 5 minutes.

5. Serve with prepared coleslaw.

Turkey Taco Lettuce Wraps

Yield: Serves 4 | Prep Time: 5 minutes | Cook Time: 20 minutes

Lettuce wraps aren't just for your gluten-free friends! They're a colorful and healthy alternative to any of your favorite wraps. I like using ground turkey, so it's almost like having an inside-out burger.

INGREDIENTS

1½ pounds lean ground turkey

1 teaspoon garlic powder

1 teaspoon cumin

1 teaspoon kosher salt

1 teaspoon chili powder

1 teaspoon paprika

½ teaspoon dried oregano

½ small onion, finely diced

1 (4-ounce) can tomato sauce

8 large iceberg lettuce leaves

¼ cup light sour cream

½ cup shredded reduced-fat Mexican-blend cheese

1 avocado, diced

1 tomato, diced

¼ cup finely chopped fresh cilantro

DIRECTIONS

1. Heat a large skillet over medium heat. Add the turkey and brown for 2 to 3 minutes. Add the garlic powder, cumin, salt, chili powder, paprika, and oregano. Stir to combine and continue browning the meat. Add the onion, ¾ cup water, and the tomato sauce and cover. Reduce the heat to low and simmer for about 20 minutes.

2. Divide the meat equally among the 8 lettuce leaves. Place a portion of the meat mixture in the center of each leaf and top with sour cream, cheese, avocado, tomato, and cilantro.

3. Serve immediately.

Greek Turkey Burgers

Yield: Serves 4 | Prep Time: 20 minutes | Cook Time: 10 minutes

Who doesn't love to indulge in a big, juicy hamburger? I certainly do, but I always feel so guilty after. This turkey version is a healthier substitute, with plenty of hidden veggies, lean turkey meat, and lighter Greek yogurt dressing. Burgers like these don't just have to be limited to an "every once in a while" kind of meal.

INGREDIENTS

1 English cucumber

¼ cup crumbled feta cheese

7 ounces plain Greek yogurt

Juice of ½ lemon

2 teaspoons chopped fresh dill

1 teaspoon minced garlic

Salt and pepper

2 ounces frozen spinach, thawed

½ red onion

1 pound ground turkey

6 sun-dried tomatoes, chopped

1 large egg

¼ cup panko bread crumbs

1 teaspoon dried oregano

4 whole wheat hamburger buns

Lettuce, for serving

Sliced tomato, for serving

DIRECTIONS

1. Grate the cucumber over a tea towel. Squeeze out as much liquid as possible.

2. In a bowl, combine the grated cucumber, feta cheese, yogurt, lemon juice, dill, ½ teaspoon of the minced garlic, and a pinch of salt. Stir everything to combine and then refrigerate while preparing the burgers.

3. Squeeze as much moisture as possible from the frozen spinach. Roughly chop the spinach. Grate the red onion and squeeze out as much moisture as possible.

4. In a bowl, combine the ground turkey with the spinach, onion, sun-dried tomatoes, egg, panko, oregano, remaining ½ teaspoon garlic, salt, and pepper to taste. Stir everything until it is evenly combined. Shape the mixture into 4 even patties.

5. Cook the burgers on a stove top grill, in a nonstick skillet, or over an open flame for about 5 minutes on each side over medium-high heat.

6. Layer the bottom half of the bun with lettuce, a thick slice of tomato, the burger patty, and the yogurt sauce before adding the bun top. Serve.

Cheesy Turkey Shepherd's Pie

Yield: Serves 4 | Prep Time: 15 minutes | Cook Time: 45 minutes

When I was living abroad in France, I decided to spend a long weekend in London to visit a friend. The first place we went after I got off the train was a cozy pub that had the best shepherd's pie. It was a heavenly relief after hours of traveling. I wanted to make a lighter version of that dish, so I could enjoy it whenever I liked without feeling guilty.

INGREDIENTS

7 Yukon Gold potatoes, diced

Meat Filling

2 tablespoons olive oil

1 small onion, diced

1 carrot, finely diced

3 cloves garlic, minced

1 pound lean ground turkey

½ tablespoon garlic powder

½ tablespoon onion powder

½ tablespoon paprika

Salt and pepper

¼ cup low-sodium beef broth

1 cup frozen peas

1 tablespoon cornstarch

Potato Topping

4 tablespoons unsalted butter, melted

¼ cup 2% milk

4 ounces low-fat cream cheese, room temperature

1 cup shredded reduced-fat sharp cheddar cheese

½ cup shredded reduced-fat mozzarella cheese

DIRECTIONS

1. Preheat the oven to 400°F. Coat an 8 × 8-inch baking dish with cooking spray and set aside.

2. Place the potatoes in a large pot and cover with cold water. Place on the stove over high heat and bring to a boil. Cook until the potatoes are tender, about 10 minutes.

3. *For the meat filling:* In a large skillet, heat the olive oil over medium heat. Add the onion and carrot. Sauté for 5 minutes, add the garlic, and cook for an additional minute.

4. Add the ground turkey, garlic powder, onion powder, paprika, and salt, and pepper to taste. Cook the turkey for about 10 minutes, add the broth, and cook for an additional 5 minutes. Add the frozen peas and stir to combine. In a small bowl, whisk together the cornstarch with 1 tablespoon water, add to the ground turkey, and cook a few minutes more to thicken the sauce.

5. *For the potato topping:* Drain the potatoes and return them to the pot. Add the melted butter and milk and mash until creamy. Add the cream cheese and stir to combine. In a small bowl, combine the cheddar cheese and mozzarella cheese. Mix half of the cheddar-mozzarella blend into the potatoes.

6. Add the meat to the casserole dish. Top with the potatoes, then with the remaining cheese blend. Bake for about 15 minutes.

7. Remove from the oven and allow to sit for 10 minutes before serving.

Dump 'n' Go Italian Meatloaf

Yield: Serves 6 | Prep Time: 10 minutes | Cook Time: 6 hours on Low or 3 hours on High

I was picking up some produce from the grocery store when I saw there was a sale on the most perfect zucchini I had ever seen. I knew I needed to buy a few and that I'd figure out how to use them later. When I was making meatloaf the next day, I saw the zucchini and decided to add them into the mix. Boy, was I thrilled with how it turned out!

INGREDIENTS

2 pounds lean ground sirloin

2 large eggs

1 zucchini, grated and excess liquid squeezed out

½ cup freshly grated Parmesan cheese

½ cup fresh parsley, finely chopped, plus extra, for garnish

4 cloves garlic, minced

1 tablespoon dried oregano

1 tablespoon onion powder

Salt and pepper

½ cup jarred marinara sauce

½ cup shredded reduced-fat mozzarella cheese

DIRECTIONS

1. Line the insert of a 6-quart slow cooker with aluminum foil. Coat the foil with cooking spray.

2. In a large bowl, combine the ground sirloin, eggs, zucchini, Parmesan cheese, parsley, garlic, oregano, onion powder, and salt and pepper to taste.

3. Carefully transfer the mixture into the slow cooker and form it into an oblong-shaped loaf, setting it on top of the aluminum foil.

4. Cover and cook for 6 hours on Low or for 3 hours on High. When you have 15 minutes left, turn off the heat and unplug the slow cooker. Remove the cover and spread the marinara sauce over the top of the meatloaf. Sprinkle the cheese on top of the sauce and replace the cover. Allow the meatloaf to sit for 5 to 10 minutes or until the cheese has melted.

5. Lift the foil to remove the meatloaf. Transfer the loaf to a serving platter and garnish with fresh parsley. Slice and serve.

Healthy Beef and Broccoli

Yield: Serves 4 | Prep Time: 15 minutes | Cook Time: 25 minutes

This dish cuts back on the amount of sodium found in the soy sauce, which helps make this a much more guilt-free version of a favorite takeout dish. If you're having trouble cutting through the slippery raw steak, throw it in the freezer for a few minutes to firm it up and try again.

INGREDIENTS

1 tablespoon olive oil

1 pound flank steak, thinly sliced across the grain

3 cloves garlic, minced

1 shallot, finely chopped

4 scallions, thinly sliced

4 cups broccoli florets

2 tablespoons cornstarch

⅓ cup low-sodium soy sauce

2 tablespoons light brown sugar

1 teaspoon minced fresh ginger

¼ teaspoon crushed red pepper flakes (adjust to desired heat level)

Toasted sesame seeds, for garnish

Quinoa, for serving

DIRECTIONS

1. In a large skillet, heat the oil over medium-high heat. Add the steak and cook until well browned, 3 to 4 minutes on each side. Once well browned, remove from the pan and set aside.

2. To the same pan, add the garlic, shallot, and scallions. Cook for 1 minute, stirring frequently. Add the broccoli, cover, and cook for an additional 5 minutes.

3. In a small bowl, whisk together the cornstarch and ¾ cup water. Add the soy sauce, brown sugar, ginger, and red pepper flakes. Set aside.

4. Remove the cover from the pan and add the sauce. Cook until the sauce starts to thicken, 3 to 5 minutes. Add the steak and stir to combine, cooking for an additional 2 to 3 minutes.

5. Top with sesame seeds and serve over quinoa, if desired.

NOTES

To cook the quinoa, put 2 cups water per 1 cup quinoa in a saucepan over high heat. Add salt. Once the water is boiling, lower the heat to low, cover, and cook for 15 minutes. Remove from the heat and let stand, covered, for 5 minutes. Serve.

Zucchini Lasagna

Yield: Serves 8 | Prep Time: 15 minutes | Cook Time: 1½ hours

The most important part of this recipe is making sure you've absorbed as much of the moisture from the zucchini as you can. Be sure to blot well with the paper towels. Plus, you can make this ahead of time and store it in the freezer for up to 2 or 3 months to reheat on a day when you don't feel like cooking.

INGREDIENTS

1 pound lean ground beef

Salt and pepper

1 teaspoon olive oil

½ large onion, chopped

3 cloves garlic, minced

1 (28-ounce) can crushed tomatoes

2 tablespoons chopped fresh basil

3 zucchini, sliced ⅛-inch thick

1½ cups part-skim ricotta cheese

¼ cup shredded Parmesan cheese

1 large egg

4 cups shredded part-skim mozzarella cheese

DIRECTIONS

1. In a medium saucepan, brown the ground beef and season with salt and pepper. Drain the excess fat and remove to a bowl. Set aside.

2. Add the olive oil to the pan and sauté the onion and garlic for about 2 minutes. Return the meat to the pan and add the tomatoes and basil. Season with salt and pepper again. Simmer on low for at least 30 to 40 minutes, covered.

3. Meanwhile, lay the zucchini slices out on paper towels. Sprinkle with salt and set aside for 10 minutes. After 10 minutes, blot any excess moisture with additional paper towels.

4. Preheat the oven to 375°F. Lightly coat a 9 × 13-inch baking dish with cooking spray.

5. In a medium bowl, mix the ricotta cheese, Parmesan cheese, and egg. Stir well.

6. Spread ½ cup of the meat sauce on the bottom of the baking dish and layer the zucchini to cover. Spread ½ cup of the ricotta cheese mixture, then top with 1 cup of the mozzarella cheese and repeat the process until all ingredients are used, approximately three layers. Top the last layer with the remaining zucchini and sauce, cover with foil, and bake for 30 minutes. Remove the foil and bake for an additional 20 minutes, then top with the remaining 1 cup mozzarella and bake until melted, about 10 minutes.

7. Let stand for 5 to 10 minutes before serving.

Spicy Slow Cooker Beef with Bell Pepper

Yield: Serves 8 | Prep Time: 20 minutes | Cook Time: 3 hours on High

By making this recipe in the slow cooker instead of on the stovetop, you can cut back on a lot of unnecessary calories. Since this takes about 3 hours to cook, I can throw it together, run a few errands, and come back to dinner ready to go.

INGREDIENTS

2 pounds lean beef chuck, thinly sliced

2 cups coarsely chopped red bell pepper

2 cups coarsely chopped green bell pepper

½ onion, sliced

2 cloves garlic, chopped

Salt and pepper, to taste

1 cup low-sodium beef broth

Sriracha sauce

2 tablespoons cornstarch

Cooked brown rice, for serving

DIRECTIONS

1. Lightly spray the insert of a 6-quart slow cooker with cooking spray.

2. Place the beef on the bottom of the slow cooker. Top with the bell peppers and onion. Sprinkle with the garlic, salt, and pepper.

3. Mix the broth with the sriracha sauce. Pour over the peppers and beef.

4. Cover and cook for 3 hours on High.

5. Mix the cornstarch with ½ cup water in a saucepan. Add 1 cup of the liquid from the meat and pepper mixture and cook on medium heat until boiling. Return this mixture to the meat and bell peppers.

6. Serve hot over brown rice.

Stuffed Spaghetti Squash

Yield: Serves 8 | Prep Time: 20 minutes | Cook Time: 40–50 minutes

Spaghetti squash is an easy (and nutritious) replacement for standard pasta. The first time I made this, my nephew was visiting and wanted to know how he could help with dinner. I gave him the spaghetti squash and fork and asked him to create all of the "noodles." He thought it was the coolest thing and didn't even mind that the pasta didn't come from a box.

INGREDIENTS

1 (3-pound) spaghetti squash

1 pound lean ground beef

1 onion, diced

8 cremini mushrooms, halved lengthwise and sliced crosswise

3 cloves garlic, minced

1 (28-ounce) can diced tomatoes, drained

1 green bell pepper, diced

Salt and freshly ground black pepper

1 teaspoon dried oregano

½ teaspoon dried thyme

¼ teaspoon cayenne pepper

Parmesan cheese, for topping (optional)

DIRECTIONS

1. Preheat the oven to 400°F. Puncture the spaghetti squash randomly with a sharp knife to allow steam to be released. Place on a baking sheet and bake for 30 to 40 minutes or until a knife can pierce the skin easily. Allow to cool and slice in half. Remove the seeds. Using a fork, scrape inside the squash to create the spaghetti "noodles."

2. While the squash is baking, prepare the filling.

3. Heat a large frying pan over medium-high heat. Add the beef, onion, mushrooms, and garlic. Cook until the meat is browned, about 6 minutes.

4. Mix in the tomatoes, bell pepper, and salt and black pepper to taste. Sprinkle with the oregano, thyme, and cayenne pepper. Reduce the heat and simmer for 10 minutes.

5. Lower the oven temperature to 350°F. Ladle the sauce on top of your prepared squash halves. Sprinkle with Parmesan cheese, if desired. Bake for 10 minutes, or until heated through and the cheese is melted. Serve.

Grilled Pineapple Teriyaki Pork Chops

Yield: Serves 4 | Prep Time: 10 minutes plus 2 hours chill time | Cook Time: 15 minutes

Teriyaki sauce is usually loaded up with soy sauce, which is high in sodium. By substituting orange juice for most of that soy sauce, you make the dish much healthier.

INGREDIENTS

¼ cup orange juice

2 tablespoons soy sauce

1 tablespoon rice vinegar

1 tablespoon light brown sugar

1 teaspoon grated fresh ginger

½ teaspoon onion powder

1 clove garlic, minced

4 bone-in pork chops, trimmed of fat

2 teaspoons cornstarch

2 teaspoons cold water

4 thickly sliced fresh pineapple rings

DIRECTIONS

1. In a large resealable bag, mix together the orange juice, soy sauce, rice vinegar, brown sugar, ginger, onion powder, and garlic to make a marinade.

2. Place the pork chops in the marinade. Seal the bag and chill in the refrigerator for at least 2 hours and up to overnight. If possible, turn the bag every hour or so to evenly cover the pork chops with the marinade.

3. Transfer the pork chops to a shallow dish. Pour the marinade into a small saucepan.

4. In a small bowl, dissolve the cornstarch in the cold water to make a slurry. Place the saucepan of marinade over medium heat and bring to a boil. Reduce the heat to low and whisk in the slurry. Cook, whisking, until the sauce thickens, about 2 minutes. Remove from the heat and set aside to use as a baste for the grilled pork chops and pineapple.

5. Preheat an indoor grill, grill pan, or outdoor grill to medium-high heat.

6. Place the pork chops on the grill and cook until the internal temperature reaches 145°F, 4 to 5 minutes per side, brushing often with the baste as you grill.

7. Place the pineapple slices on the grill and cook for 1 to 2 minutes on each side.

8. Let the pork chops rest for 2 to 4 minutes before serving.

9. To serve, place one grilled pineapple slice on top of each pork chop.

Garlic Roasted Pork Chops

Yield: Serves 4 | Prep Time: 10 minutes | Cook Time: 15 minutes

Sometimes the simplest recipes are among the best. I can never remember if I have garlic at home, so I usually wind up buying several bulbs every time I go to the grocery store. When I start to feel overwhelmed by the number of extra garlic bulbs I have, I like to make this dish to work my way through them.

INGREDIENTS

4 bone-in pork chops, about 1 inch thick

2 teaspoons salt

1 teaspoon freshly ground black pepper

6 cloves garlic, peeled and left whole

2 tablespoons olive oil

Fresh parsley, for garnish

DIRECTIONS

1. Preheat the oven to 400°F. Line a baking sheet with foil.

2. Season both sides of the pork chops well with the salt and pepper. Place on the baking sheet along with the whole garlic cloves. Drizzle all with the olive oil.

3. Place the baking sheet in the oven and roast for 10 to 15 minutes, or until the chops are cooked through and no longer pink.

4. Remove from the oven. Allow the chops to rest for about 5 minutes and then serve. Serve the roasted garlic alongside and garnish with parsley.

Healthy Slow Cooker Pulled Pork

Yield: Serves 8–10 | Prep Time: 20 minutes | Cook Time: 8–10 hours on Low

Most pulled pork recipes utilize a bottle or two of barbecue sauce to add flavor to the meat. By eliminating the sauce and using spices, tomato paste, and vinegar instead, you can cut back on the sugars and artificial preservatives while maintaining a flavorful dish.

INGREDIENTS

1 (4- to 6-pound) boneless pork shoulder roast

1 large onion, diced

4 cloves garlic, crushed

¼ cup apple cider vinegar

3 tablespoons tomato paste

3 tablespoons maple syrup

2 tablespoons chili powder

Salt and pepper

8–10 whole wheat buns

Prepared coleslaw, for serving

DIRECTIONS

1. Use paper towels to pat the pork shoulder dry. Place the shoulder into an 8.5-quart slow cooker. Add the onion and garlic. Stir in the apple cider vinegar, tomato paste, maple syrup, chili powder, and salt and pepper to taste.

2. Cover and cook for 8 to 10 hours on Low or until the meat is very tender and easily shreds.

3. Use two forks to pull the meat apart, then stir it into the cooking juices.

4. Season with salt and pepper, to taste.

5. Serve on a whole wheat bun with coleslaw.

Low-Carb Jalapeño Popper Pork Chops

Yield: Serves 4 | Prep Time: 20 minutes | Cook Time: 10 minutes

While spices are often used to make a dish flavorful without the unnecessary preservatives found in many sauces and dressings, another trick is to add hot peppers. The sauce's main job is to diversify the flavors of the dish, and when you can add something with fewer calories into the mix, like jalapeños, you can achieve the same effect.

INGREDIENTS

4 bone-in pork chops

1 teaspoon garlic powder

1 teaspoon kosher salt

¼ teaspoon freshly ground black pepper

1 tablespoon olive oil

6 ounces low-fat cream cheese, softened

½ cup salsa verde

¼ cup shredded reduced-fat cheddar cheese

1 jalapeño, chopped

⅓ cup chopped cooked bacon (optional)

DIRECTIONS

1. Preheat a grill to medium-high heat. Alternatively, preheat a grill pan over medium-high heat on the stovetop.

2. Sprinkle the pork chops with the garlic powder, salt, and pepper. Drizzle with the olive oil.

3. In a small bowl, combine the cream cheese, salsa verde, half the cheddar cheese, and half the chopped jalapeño. Set aside.

4. Once the grill is hot, grill the pork chops for 3 to 4 minutes per side or until just cooked through.

5. Divide the cheese mixture between the chops and spoon it on top.

6. Top with the remaining cheddar cheese, chopped jalapeños, and chopped bacon (if desired). Serve.

5

Seafood, Pasta, and Vegetarian

Growing up in the Midwest, it took me a while before I "got" the fuss about seafood. Minnesota isn't exactly close to the ocean! The best part is that seafood is rich in nutrients and lower in calories than red meat, which means you can enjoy many favorites like Skinny Tuna Noodle Casserole (page 136) or Low Country Boil (page 128) without making too many adjustments from the original version. Pasta, on the other hand, is the ideal base for many dinner ingredients. Because it doesn't have an overpowering taste on its own, it acts as a canvas for the surrounding ingredients, allowing a particular sauce to shine or drawing your attention to a smoky vegetable mixed in. The pasta and vegetarian recipes in this book run the gamut from Ravioli with Asparagus and Walnuts (page 147) to Veggie Quinoa Sushi Rolls (page 152).

Healthy Crab Mac 'n' Cheese

Yield: Serves 4–6 | Prep Time: 10 minutes | Cook Time: 30 minutes

Who doesn't love mac 'n' cheese? When I was growing up, I would often ask my parents if we could have mac 'n' cheese for dinner, and they'd tell me it wouldn't be good for us if we had it every single night. If I had suggested that we make it healthier by adding some cauliflower and crab, perhaps they would've relented a little more often.

INGREDIENTS

Cauliflower Purée

2 cups roughly chopped cauliflower

⅓ cup low-sodium chicken or vegetable broth

Crab Mixture

1 tablespoon unsalted butter

½ cup red bell pepper, chopped

¼ cup chopped celery

¼ cup chopped onion

Salt and pepper

1 clove garlic, minced

1 (8-ounce) can refrigerated crabmeat, picked through for shells

2 tablespoons chopped fresh parsley

1 teaspoon Old Bay seasoning

Zest of 1 lemon

Mac 'n' Cheese

3½ cups cooked macaroni (about 2 cups dry)

2 cups bite-size pieces steamed cauliflower

1⅓ cups shredded reduced-fat cheddar cheese

Salt

A couple of tablespoons low-sodium chicken broth, if needed

⅓ cup panko bread crumbs

DIRECTIONS

1. *For the cauliflower purée:* In a large microwave-safe bowl, place the cauliflower and chicken broth. Cover with plastic wrap and microwave on high for 5 to 7 minutes, until the cauliflower is very tender. Carefully transfer to a blender and pulse until smooth. Measure out 1 cup of purée and set aside the remainder for another use.

2. *For the crab mixture:* Preheat the oven to 350°F. Coat an 8 × 8-inch baking dish with cooking spray.

3. Meanwhile, heat a large skillet over medium heat, add the butter, and cook until it melts. Add the bell pepper, celery, and onion, seasoning lightly with salt and pepper. Cook the veggies until softened, about 4 minutes.

4. Add the garlic and let cook for an additional 1 to 2 minutes. Gently stir in the crabmeat, parsley, Old Bay seasoning, and lemon zest. Transfer the mixture to a large bowl.

5. *For the mac 'n' cheese:* Add the cooked macaroni, cauliflower purée, chopped cauliflower, cheddar cheese, and a pinch of salt to the crab mixture. Stir until the cheese is melted and everything is combined. Add chicken broth if the mixture seems too dry. Pour the mixture into the baking dish. Sprinkle the panko over the top and lightly coat with cooking spray.

6. Bake for 15 minutes, uncovered, until the bread crumbs are golden brown and everything is bubbling. Serve.

Low Country Boil

Yield: Serves 4–6 | Prep Time: 5 minutes | Cook Time: 15 minutes

You don't always need a ton of sauces or condiments to make an appealing recipe. Sometimes when you go back to the basics, like we have with this Louisiana staple, you can get a dish everyone will appreciate while sticking to a clean-eating diet, devoid of unnecessary sauces and added preservatives.

INGREDIENTS

1 pound small potatoes, halved and whole (I used red and Yukon Gold)

1 lemon, sliced

¼ cup Old Bay seasoning

1 pound andouille sausage, cut into 2-inch pieces

4 ears fresh corn, cut into thirds

2 pounds fresh shrimp with shells on

Cocktail sauce, for serving

Melted unsalted butter, for serving

DIRECTIONS

1. Quarter the potatoes and add to a very large pot with at least 6 cups water. Bring to a boil over high heat. Boil for 5 minutes. Add the lemon, Old Bay seasoning, sausage, and corn. Continue to boil until the potatoes are tender and the corn is cooked. Add the shrimp and cook just until the shrimp turn pink.

2. Remove from the heat and carefully drain. Remove the lemon and return everything else to the pot.

3. Serve with cocktail sauce and melted butter, if desired.

Cilantro Lime Black Bean Shrimp and Rice

Yield: Serves 4 | Prep Time: 10 minutes | Cook Time: 30 minutes

Brown jasmine rice is much higher in fiber than white rice, which is what makes this such an appealing choice for a healthy meal. The touch of red pepper complements the combination of cilantro and lime juice perfectly for a light yet flavorful dish.

INGREDIENTS

1 cup uncooked brown jasmine rice

2 cups low-sodium chicken broth

2 tablespoons olive oil

4 cloves garlic, minced

½ teaspoon red pepper flakes

Salt and pepper

1 (15-ounce) can black beans, rinsed and drained

½ cup fresh cilantro, chopped, plus extra for serving

2 tablespoons fresh lime juice, plus extra for serving

1 pound raw shrimp, peeled and deveined

DIRECTIONS

1. Heat a large skillet over medium heat. Pour the jasmine rice inside. Add the chicken broth, olive oil, garlic, and red pepper flakes. Season with salt and pepper and mix. Bring to a boil. Lower the heat to a low simmer. Cover the skillet with the lid. Simmer for 15 to 20 minutes, covered, until the rice is cooked through.

2. Mix the black beans, cilantro, and lime juice into the cooked rice. Season the shrimp with salt and pepper and nestle it into the cooked rice. Cover and cook just until the shrimp are pink and beginning to curl, about 10 minutes.

3. Add extra lime juice and extra chopped fresh cilantro to the plate when serving.

Low-Carb Teriyaki Salmon

Yield: Serves 4 | Prep Time: 5 minutes | Cook Time: 15 minutes

I've heard countless times that salmon is chock-full of omega-3s, but for the longest time, I really didn't know what that meant. Apparently, omega-3s may help prevent heart disease and improve brain function. I've paired the salmon here with a side of *goma-ae*, a Japanese side dish that's chock-full of nutrients, too.

INGREDIENTS

4 (6-ounce) salmon fillets

¼ cup low-sodium teriyaki sauce, plus more for brushing

1 teaspoon toasted sesame seeds

Goma-Ae

2 cups spinach

1 tablespoon dashi

1 teaspoon soy sauce

½ teaspoon sugar

⅓ cup toasted sesame seeds

⅛ teaspoon salt

DIRECTIONS

1. Preheat the broiler on high heat and position a rack 3 to 4 inches below the flame. Line a large baking sheet with foil and coat it with cooking spray.

2. Place the salmon pieces on the foil. Brush the salmon with teriyaki sauce. Broil for 5 to 6 minutes, or until opaque.

3. Transfer the salmon fillets onto a serving platter. Brush with additional teriyaki sauce and sprinkle with the sesame seeds.

4. *For the goma-ae:* Bring a large pot of water to a boil and prepare a bowl of ice water.

5. Add the spinach to the boiling water and cook for 2 minutes or until cooked through. Drain, rinse briefly with cool water, and then momentarily add to the ice water.

6. Remove the spinach and squeeze out as much water as you can. Cut into 2-inch pieces.

7. In a medium bowl, combine the dashi, soy sauce, and sugar. Add the spinach and toss well to distribute.

8. Grind the sesame seeds and salt in a food processor or blender. Add to the spinach and stir. Serve on the side of the salmon.

20-Minute Lemon, Garlic, and Herb Baked Cod

Yield: Serves 4 | Prep Time: 5 minutes | Cook Time: 15 minutes

Cod is the fish I tend to cook for friends or family members who claim they don't like fish. Its flavor is less "fishy" than other species and tends to go over better with a fish-fearful crowd. The addition of sweet, creamy Greek yogurt helps add texture and flavor without unnecessary preservatives.

INGREDIENTS

4 (8-ounce) Alaskan cod fillets

1 cup panko bread crumbs

1 tablespoon olive oil

⅓ cup plain Greek yogurt

¼ cup fresh parsley, chopped

¼ cup fresh basil, chopped

3 tablespoons grated Parmesan cheese

2 cloves garlic, grated or finely minced

Zest and juice of 1 large lemon

Salt and pepper

Romaine leaves, for serving

DIRECTIONS

1. Preheat the oven to 400°F. Line a large baking sheet with parchment paper. Place the cod fillets on the sheet and set aside.

2. In a small bowl, combine the panko and olive oil and toss well to evenly coat.

3. In another bowl, combine the Greek yogurt, parsley, basil, Parmesan cheese, garlic, lemon zest, lemon juice, salt, and pepper. Spoon one-quarter of the yogurt mixture on top of each fillet and then dip each fillet into the panko mixture, coating all sides.

4. Bake until firm, 12 to 15 minutes, depending on the thickness of the fish. Serve over Romaine, with additional lemon if desired.

Skinny Tuna Noodle Casserole

Yield: Serves 6 | Prep Time: 10 minutes | Cook Time: 55 minutes

Sometimes the easiest way to lighten up a favorite recipe is just to find low-fat versions of the original ingredients. You can cut back on unneeded calories while maintaining the ideal combination of ingredients. I also like adding in mushrooms, peas, and onions to get a full helping of veggies in each serving of this casserole.

INGREDIENTS

6 ounces no-yolk egg noodles

1 tablespoon unsalted butter

1 onion, finely minced

3 tablespoons all-purpose flour

Salt and pepper

1½ cups fat-free chicken broth

1 cup 2% milk

10 ounces sliced white button mushrooms

1 cup frozen petite peas

2 (5-ounce) cans tuna in water, drained

1 cup reduced-fat sharp cheddar cheese

¼ cup grated Parmesan cheese

¼ cup panko bread crumbs

DIRECTIONS

1. Bring a large pot of water to a boil. Add the egg noodles and cook until 2 minutes shy of al dente. Drain and return the pasta to the pot.

2. Preheat the oven to 375°F. Lightly coat a 9 × 13-inch baking dish with cooking spray. Set aside.

3. Melt the butter in a large, deep skillet over medium heat. Add the onion and cook until soft, about 5 minutes. Lower the heat to medium-low.

4. Add the flour and a pinch of salt and stir well, cooking for an additional 2 to 3 minutes.

5. Slowly whisk in the chicken broth until well combined, increasing the heat to medium and whisking well for 30 seconds. Then add the milk and bring to a boil.

6. When boiling, add the mushrooms and peas, and season with salt and pepper to taste, and simmer on medium, mixing occasionally, until it thickens, 7 to 9 minutes.

7. Add the drained tuna, stirring for another minute.

8. Remove from the heat, add the cheddar cheese, and mix well until it melts. Add the noodles to the sauce and mix well until evenly coated.

9. Pour into the baking dish and top with the Parmesan cheese and panko. Spray a little more cooking spray on top and bake for about 25 minutes. Slice and serve.

One-Skillet Seafood Alfredo

Yield: Serves 4 | Prep Time: 5 minutes | Cook Time: 20 minutes

While fish is a healthy addition to any diet, there can be plenty of calories hidden in any cream-based dressings. To make this dish lighter, we've substituted a combination of chicken broth, 2% milk, and flour for heavy cream. That way, you're still able to achieve that thick, creamy texture that's indicative of an Alfredo dish while cutting out the unhealthier elements.

INGREDIENTS

1½ cups uncooked regular, whole-wheat, or gluten-free mini penne pasta

Salt and pepper, to taste

2 tablespoons olive oil

¼ cup minced onion

2 tablespoons minced garlic

¾ cup low-sodium chicken broth

¾ cup 2% milk

1 tablespoon all-purpose flour

1 (8-ounce) package Louis Kemp Crab Delights imitation crabmeat

½ pound peeled, deveined, and cooked shrimp

1 cup freshly grated Parmesan cheese

Fresh parsley, chopped, for garnish

Scallion, chopped, for garnish

DIRECTIONS

1. Bring a large pot of water to a boil. Add the penne pasta and salt and cook until al dente. Drain and return the pasta to the pot.

2. Heat the olive oil in a skillet over medium-high heat. Add the onion and garlic and cook for 1 minute, stirring constantly.

3. Add the chicken broth, milk, and flour to the onion and whisk until completely combined. Cook until the mixture thickens slightly.

4. Stir in the cooked pasta, crabmeat, and shrimp and cook for an additional 2 to 3 minutes, or until the seafood is heated through.

5. Remove from the heat and stir in the Parmesan cheese.

6. Season with salt and pepper, if needed. Garnish with the parsley and scallion. Serve immediately.

Baked Tilapia

Yield: Serves 4 | Prep Time: 5 minutes | Cook Time: 20 minutes

The lemon-garlic topping is my favorite part of this dish because the tartness of the lemon adds a refreshing kick against the spice-infused fish. I'd recommend serving either Slow Cooker Garlic Mashed Cauliflower (page 169) or Roasted Parmesan Asparagus (page 170) on the side.

INGREDIENTS

2 tablespoons fresh parsley, chopped, plus more for serving

¾ teaspoon paprika

½ teaspoon dried thyme

½ teaspoon dried oregano

½ teaspoon dried basil

Salt and pepper

4 tilapia fillets

2 tablespoons unsalted butter, melted

Juice of 1 lemon

2 cloves garlic, minced

Lemon slices, for serving

DIRECTIONS

1. Preheat the oven to 350°F. Line a baking sheet with foil and coat with cooking spray. Set aside.

2. In a small bowl, combine the parsley, paprika, thyme, oregano, basil, and salt and pepper to taste.

3. Carefully sprinkle over both sides of the tilapia fillets. Place the fillets on the baking sheet.

4. In a small bowl, combine the melted butter, lemon juice, and garlic. Drizzle the lemon mixture over the fillets.

5. Bake, uncovered, for 15 to 20 minutes or until the fish flakes easily. Serve with parsley and lemon slices.

Spaghetti and Meatballs Casserole

Yield: Serves 4 | Prep Time: 20 minutes | Cook Time: 50 minutes

My mom is a big fan of spaghetti and meatballs, so when I told her that I was preparing a lighter casserole version, she was floored. She raved over how baking it gives the dish a slightly crispier quality and vowed to try it out herself the next night!

INGREDIENTS

1 (16-ounce) package regular, whole-wheat, or gluten-free spaghetti

1 tablespoon olive oil

12 premade vegetarian or turkey meatballs

1 red onion, diced

4 cloves garlic, minced

1 (8-ounce) package white button mushrooms, diced

1 (24-ounce) jar marinara sauce

Salt and pepper

½ cup sliced fresh mozzarella cheese

Fresh basil, for serving

DIRECTIONS

1. Preheat the oven to 375°F.

2. Bring a large pot of water to a boil. Add the spaghetti and cook until al dente. Drain and return the pasta to the pot.

3. Heat the oil in a large frying pan and cook the meatballs until browned, about 5 minutes. Add the onion and garlic and cook for an additional 3 to 5 minutes until the onion is tender before adding the mushrooms. Let everything cook together, stirring occasionally, for an additional 5 minutes.

4. Combine the spaghetti with the meatball mixture and the marinara sauce. If the mixture looks a bit thick, add a dash of water. Season with salt and pepper to taste.

5. Transfer the mixture to a 9 × 13-inch baking dish. Dot with the mozzarella cheese.

6. Bake for about 25 minutes, until the cheese has melted and the edges of the spaghetti are a little crispy. Serve with fresh basil.

Vegetarian Asparagus and Cauliflower Alfredo

Yield: Serves 4 | Prep Time: 10 minutes | Cook Time: 40 minutes

To make the Alfredo sauce a bit lighter, I used almond milk instead of 2%. Almond milk is incredibly nutritious with plenty of fiber, vitamin E, magnesium, and more. Plus, it adds a rich, sweet flavor to the sauce that complements the pasta and asparagus beautifully.

INGREDIENTS

Asparagus

1 bunch asparagus, trimmed

1 tablespoon olive oil

Salt and pepper

Alfredo Sauce

1 tablespoon olive oil

4 cloves garlic, minced

1 cup unsweetened almond milk

½ cup vegetable broth

Juice of 1 lemon

1 head cauliflower, chopped

Salt and pepper

Pasta

1 (16-ounce) package regular, whole-wheat, or gluten-free penne pasta

1 cup grated Parmesan cheese

DIRECTIONS

1. *For the asparagus:* Preheat the oven to 450°F and line a large rimmed baking sheet with a silicone mat or parchment paper.

2. Place the asparagus on the baking sheet and toss with the olive oil, salt, and pepper. Roast the asparagus, stirring halfway through, for 15 minutes or until it is crisp-tender and beginning to lightly brown. Remove from the oven and set aside.

3. *For the alfredo sauce:* Heat the olive oil in a large sauté pan over medium heat. Add the garlic and sauté for 30 seconds.

4. Slowly whisk in the almond milk, vegetable broth, and lemon juice and bring the mixture to a simmer. Once simmering, add the chopped cauliflower and season with salt and pepper.

5. Simmer the cauliflower for 7 to 10 minutes or until the cauliflower is soft.

6. Remove from the heat and carefully pour the mixture into a high-powered blender.

7. Blend on high until smooth, about 3 minutes. Season with salt and pepper.

8. *For the pasta:* Bring a large pot of water to a boil. Add the penne pasta and cook until al dente. Drain and return to the pot.

9. Add the roasted asparagus and the sauce.

10. Season with salt and pepper again if necessary, top with the Parmesan cheese, and serve immediately.

Ravioli with Asparagus and Walnuts

Yield: Serves 2 | Prep Time: 10 minutes | Cook Time: 10 minutes

Ravioli and tortellini are two of my favorite pastas to cook with. They already have some sort of filling—from cheese to spinach to chicken—so half the work is done for you! By adding a veggie like asparagus and a hint of sunny lemon flavor, you can turn a traditionally heavy dish into something light and refreshing. The walnuts also help improve heart function and bone health.

INGREDIENTS

3 tablespoons unsalted butter

½ pound asparagus, cut into thirds

1 (8-ounce) package fresh regular, whole-wheat, or gluten-free ravioli

Juice of 1 lemon

Salt and pepper to taste

¼ cup walnuts

2 tablespoons fresh minced parsley

2 tablespoons grated Parmesan cheese

DIRECTIONS

1. Bring a large pot of water to a boil.

2. In a large saucepan, melt the butter over medium heat. Add the chopped asparagus to the pan, stir slightly to coat the asparagus with butter, and cover with the pan with a lid. Cook for 4 minutes.

3. While the asparagus is cooking, add the ravioli to the boiling water and cook until al dente. Drain and add to a bowl.

4. When the asparagus is done, remove with a slotted spoon. Add the asparagus to the bowl of ravioli. There will be some browned butter left in the bottom of the pan.

5. Add the lemon juice to the pan and season with salt and pepper.

6. Pour the butter-lemon sauce over the cooked ravioli and asparagus.

7. Add the walnuts, parsley, and Parmesan cheese and toss gently to combine.

Skinny Lasagna Rolls

Yield: Serves 4 | Prep Time: 10 minutes | Cook Time: 40 minutes

The trick to cutting back on lasagna is to make lasagna rolls. When we are served a casserole dish full of lasagna, oftentimes, our eyes can be bigger than our stomachs as we serve ourselves an ambitious piece. With these lasagna rolls, the amount is predetermined, so you won't be tempted to overindulge, but they still offer more flexibility in preparation than tricky-to-stuff manicotti shells.

INGREDIENTS

1 (15-ounce) container fat-free ricotta cheese

1 (10-ounce) package frozen chopped spinach, thawed and drained

½ cup grated Parmesan cheese

1 large egg

Salt and pepper to taste

4 cups spaghetti sauce

9 regular, whole-wheat, or gluten-free lasagna noodles, cooked (½ of a 16-ounce package)

½ cup shredded part-skim mozzarella cheese

DIRECTIONS

1. Preheat the oven to 350°F. Lightly coat a 9 × 13-inch baking dish with cooking spray.

2. In a medium bowl, combine the ricotta cheese, spinach, Parmesan cheese, egg, salt, and pepper.

3. Evenly spread about 1 cup of the spaghetti sauce on the bottom of the baking dish.

4. Place a piece of waxed or parchment paper on the counter and lay out the lasagna noodles.

5. Spread ⅓ cup of the ricotta mixture evenly over each noodle.

6. Carefully roll up each noodle and place seam-side down into the baking dish.

7. Spoon the remaining spaghetti sauce over the noodles and top each one with 1 tablespoon of the mozzarella cheese.

8. Cover the baking dish with foil and bake for 40 minutes or until the cheese melts. Serve.

Creamy Avocado Spinach Pasta

Yield: Serves 4 | Prep Time: 10 minutes | Cook Time: 12 minutes

Avocado spinach sauce is the new hip pasta accompaniment! The best part about it is how light it feels. The avocado sauce doesn't overpower the dish but rather adds a smooth, creamy texture to a beloved pasta staple.

INGREDIENTS

1 pound regular, whole-wheat, or gluten-free fettuccine pasta

2 cups fresh spinach

1 avocado

½ cup pecans

¼ cup fresh basil

¼ cup grated Parmesan cheese

2 cloves garlic

Juice of 1 lemon

Salt and pepper to taste

DIRECTIONS

1. Bring a large pot of water to a boil. Add the fettuccine and cook until al dente. Drain, reserving 1¼ cups of the pasta water, and return the pasta plus ¼ cup of the reserved pasta water to the pot.

2. In a blender, combine 1 cup of the spinach, the avocado, pecans, basil, Parmesan cheese, garlic, lemon juice, salt, and pepper and blend on high for about 3 minutes until smooth.

3. Add the remaining 1 cup pasta water to the blender and blend on high for 1 more minute.

4. Add the sauce to the bowl of pasta along with the remaining 1 cup spinach. Toss to wilt the spinach.

5. Serve immediately.

Veggie Quinoa Sushi Rolls

Yield: Serves 2–3 | Prep Time: 15 minutes | Cook Time: 15 minutes

A couple of years ago, my girlfriends asked me to give them a cooking demonstration. They wanted something that was out-of-the-box that we could enjoy eating while watching terrible movies together. We ended up making sushi, and it was such a blast! To make sushi even healthier, I've swapped out the more traditional rice outer layer for quinoa, packing it with even more nutrition.

INGREDIENTS

1 cup uncooked quinoa

¼ teaspoon sea salt

1 tablespoon rice vinegar

2 scallions

1 carrot

1 avocado

4–5 nori sheets (see Note)

Reduced-sodium tamari sauce

Pickled ginger, for serving

NOTE

You can find nori sheets online, or in the Japanese food aisle at your grocery store.

DIRECTIONS

1. In a large saucepan, combine 2 cups water, the quinoa, and the sea salt over medium-high heat. Cover and bring to a boil. Lower to medium-low heat and simmer for about 15 minutes.

2. When the quinoa is cooked and all of the water is absorbed, remove from the heat and stir in the vinegar.

3. Allow the quinoa to cool while slicing the scallions, carrot, and avocado into long thin strips.

4. Place a nori sheet on a bamboo sushi mat and place about ⅔ cup of the quinoa in the center of the nori sheet.

5. Wet the tips of your fingers (you may wish to have a bowl of cool water nearby for this purpose) and press/spread the quinoa into a thin layer—working toward the edges of the sheet, leaving about an inch of sheet remaining on the edge farthest from you.

6. Top with a thin row of scallions, carrots, and avocado slices.

7. Moisten the far edge of the nori and use the bamboo mat to help roll the sushi.

8. Set the sushi roll aside and repeat with the remaining ingredients.

9. Once all of the ingredients have been used, slice the sushi rolls crosswise into even pieces and serve with low-sodium tamari soy sauce and pickled ginger.

Baked Zucchini Parmesan Casserole

Yield: Serves 8 | Prep Time: 20 minutes | Cook Time: 50 minutes

Chicken and eggplant Parmesan are so last year. Zucchini Parmesan is the way to go. My husband isn't a big fan of eggplant, so when I was looking for a healthier version of Chicken Parm, I challenged myself to try something different.

INGREDIENTS

2 zucchinis

5 egg whites

¾ cup seasoned Italian bread crumbs

1 pound regular, whole-wheat, or gluten-free penne pasta

2 cups canned tomato sauce

½ cup shredded low-fat mozzarella cheese

Fresh parsley, for garnish

DIRECTIONS

1. Preheat the oven to 400°F. Lightly coat a 9 × 13-inch baking dish with cooking spray.

2. Cut the zucchini into ½-inch-thick slices. Put the egg whites and bread crumbs in separate shallow bowls.

3. Dip the zucchini pieces into the egg white and then cover with the bread crumbs. Place on a baking sheet and bake for 30 minutes, carefully flipping once toward the end. Remove from the oven when browned and firm.

4. While the zucchini bakes, bring a large pot of water to a boil. Cook the penne pasta until al dente. Drain and mix together with 2 cups of the tomato sauce and ½ cup of the mozzarella cheese. Pour into the baking dish.

5. Arrange the baked zucchini pieces over the top. Bake for 10 minutes or until the cheese is melting and everything is hot and bubbling.

6. Sprinkle with parsley and serve.

Zucchini and Herbed Ricotta Flatbread

Yield: Serves 6–8 | Prep Time: 1 hour | Cook Time: 40 minutes

Pizza is one of those foods that tends to break me from my diet. If I go into work and see leftover pizza up for grabs, I can't help but sneak a slice. This veggie version saves me from giving in to temptation because I can satisfy my pizza cravings and still stay on a healthier track. Not to mention, the goat cheese adds more nutrients to the dish than mozzarella cheese would.

INGREDIENTS

1 premade refrigerated whole-wheat pizza crust

2 cups halved multicolor cherry tomatoes

2 tablespoons olive oil

Salt and pepper

2 cups ricotta cheese

3 tablespoons chopped fresh basil

2 tablespoons 2% milk

1 tablespoon fresh lemon juice

4 cloves garlic, minced

1 zucchini, sliced

2 (3.5-ounce) containers crumbled goat cheese

DIRECTIONS

1. Thaw the refrigerated dough to room temperature. Preheat the oven to 400°F.

2. In a medium bowl, toss the halved cherry tomatoes with 1 tablespoon of the olive oil and a sprinkle of salt and pepper. Spread the tomatoes onto a baking sheet lined with parchment paper or a silicone baking mat and bake for about 20 minutes until blistered and roasted. Set aside.

3. Turn the oven up to 475°F.

4. In a medium bowl, whisk the ricotta, basil, milk, lemon juice, and garlic together. Add salt and pepper to taste.

5. Divide the dough into two portions. On a lightly floured surface, use a rolling pin to shape the dough into an oval until it is ¼ inch thick. Repeat with the second piece of dough. Carefully transfer both pieces of dough to a baking sheet lined with parchment paper or a silicone baking mat (or use a pizza stone).

6. Drizzle each crust with the remaining 1 tablespoon olive oil. Spread half of the ricotta mixture onto each, then top with the zucchini and tomatoes. Sprinkle the goat cheese on top of each.

7. Bake for 15 to 20 minutes or until the crust and toppings are browned to your liking. Remove from the oven and sprinkle with salt and pepper.

Low-Carb Cauliflower Pizza

Yield: Serves 2–4 | Prep Time: 5 minutes | Cook Time: 25 minutes

Traditional crusts, meet your competition. Cauliflower crusts are here to stay. The flavor isn't overpowering, which allows the juicy tomato and the melty cheese to really shine through. For this version, I didn't add any other toppings aside from cheese, but feel free to add pepperoni, mushrooms, sausage, and more to suit your tastes.

INGREDIENTS

1 head cauliflower, cut into thick slices

2 tablespoons olive oil

Salt and pepper

6 slices mozzarella cheese, cut to fit the cauliflower

1 large tomato, sliced

Fresh basil, chopped, for serving (optional)

DIRECTIONS

1. Preheat the oven to 400°F. Line a baking sheet with parchment paper.

2. Place the cauliflower slices on the baking sheet. Drizzle with the oil and season with salt and pepper. Bake for about 20 minutes until slightly crispy around the edges.

3. Top the cauliflower with a layer of cheese slices followed by a layer of tomato. Return to the oven for an additional 5 minutes until the cheese has melted and is slightly crispy.

4. Serve topped with fresh basil, if desired.

Portobello Fajitas

Yield: Serves 6 | Prep Time: 10 minutes | Cook Time: 10 minutes

Portobello mushrooms are severely underrated. They're low in calories, cholesterol, and fat while still providing important nutrients like potassium and vitamin D and giving you that hearty, satisfying edge. They take the place of beef or chicken in this recipe, so it's perfect for serving to your vegetarian friends.

INGREDIENTS

Seasoning

1 tablespoon chili powder

1 teaspoon dried oregano

1 teaspoon onion powder

1 teaspoon garlic powder

1 teaspoon paprika

½ teaspoon cumin

½ teaspoon salt

½ teaspoon lemon pepper

¼ teaspoon cayenne pepper

Filling

1 tablespoon olive oil

1 green bell pepper, sliced

8 mini bell peppers, sliced, plus additional whole bell peppers for garnish, if desired

1 onion, chopped

6 large portobello mushrooms, trimmed and sliced

1 tablespoon lime juice

Salt and pepper

6 corn tortillas

Avocados, sour cream, and shredded cheese, for serving (optional)

DIRECTIONS

1. *For the seasoning:* In a large bowl, combine the chili powder, oregano, onion powder, garlic powder, paprika, cumin, salt, lemon pepper, and cayenne pepper.

2. *For the filling:* In a large skillet, heat the olive oil over medium heat. Add the bell peppers and onion. Cook for about 2 minutes.

3. Add the mushrooms and seasoning mix. Stirring occasionally, cook for another 7 to 8 minutes or until softened. Add the lime juice, season with salt and pepper, and turn off the heat.

4. Spoon the fajita mixture into the center of the tortilla, and serve with toppings of your choice, like avocados, sour cream, and shredded cheese.

6

Sides

Side dishes can make or break a meal. You go out to a restaurant and order the light and healthy chicken sandwich, but when the waiter asks you if you'd like a side of salad or fries, you come to a crossroads. My goal with this chapter was to find a group of sides that wouldn't make you miss those salty, greasy fries. Stay on track with options such as Zucchini Tots (page 174) and Roasted Parmesan Asparagus (page 170).

Noodle Salad with Sesame Garlic Dressing

Yield: Serves 10 | Prep Time: 10 minutes | Cook Time: 10 minutes

We had a potluck luncheon in our office one day where everyone brought in a side dish. We all just picked bits of this and that to fill us up for the day. I made this noodle salad, and it was such a hit! The cold, crunchy, mayonnaise-free coleslaw really popped against the savory dressing and had a few people asking me to share the recipe.

INGREDIENTS

Dressing

⅓ cup teriyaki sauce

⅓ cup olive oil

¼ cup packed dark brown sugar

4 cloves garlic, minced

2 tablespoons Thai sweet chili sauce

Salad

1 (12.8-ounce) package chow mein or soba noodles

2 cups mayonnaise-free coleslaw mix

½ onion, finely diced

8 large radishes, sliced

DIRECTIONS

1. *For the dressing:* Place the teriyaki sauce, oil, brown sugar, garlic, and chili sauce in a blender and process until smooth. Cover and chill until ready to use.

2. *For the salad:* Bring a small pot of water to a boil.

3. Place the noodles into a large bowl and cover with the boiling water. Set aside for about 5 minutes to cook.

4. Drain the noodles and, if you wish, cut them so they are a little bit shorter and easier to deal with.

5. Add the coleslaw mix, onion, and radishes. Toss to combine.

6. Drizzle with the dressing and toss to distribute evenly. Chill until ready to serve.

Back-to-Basics Broccoli Salad

Yield: Serves 8 | Prep Time: 10 minutes | Cook Time: 16 minutes

I usually feel great about getting my share of veggies in when I have broccoli salad, until I remember that it's probably loaded with way too much mayonnaise. In order to make a broccoli salad recipe I actually felt good about, I wanted to see if I could make a version that used yogurt to replace part of the mayonnaise. And it worked!

INGREDIENTS

1 tablespoon kosher salt, plus ½ teaspoon

2 cups frozen peas

1 pound fresh cauliflower, cut into bite-size pieces

1 pound fresh broccoli, cut into bite-size pieces

6 slices bacon, chopped

½ cup light mayonnaise

½ cup low-fat plain yogurt

1 cup shredded reduced-fat mozzarella cheese

DIRECTIONS

1. In a large pot, bring water and 1 tablespoon of the salt to a boil. Drop the peas into the water for 3 minutes, then remove with a slotted spoon or wire-mesh sieve.

2. In the same boiling water, boil the cauliflower for 3 minutes. Lift it out with a slotted spoon and run it under cold water to cool.

3. In the same boiling water, boil the broccoli for 2 minutes. Lift it out as with the cauliflower and run it under cold water to cool.

4. In a small frying pan, cook the bacon over medium heat until browned and lightly crisp, about 8 minutes. Drain well on paper towels.

5. In a small bowl, combine the mayonnaise, yogurt, and remaining ½ teaspoon salt to create a dressing.

6. When the vegetables have cooled, toss with the dressing. Taste for seasoning. Add the bacon and mozzarella cheese, and stir gently until well mixed.

7. Serve immediately or cover and chill in the refrigerator until ready to eat.

Slow Cooker Garlic Mashed Cauliflower

Yield: Serves 6 | Prep Time: 5 minutes | Cook Time: 6 hours on Low or 3 hours on High

I have nothing against potatoes. When the holidays roll around, I serve a minimum of three different types of potatoes—and that's only after my husband's convinced me to abandon a few others. This cauliflower alternative is so easy because it still has that soft, fluffy texture everyone loves, but it isn't nearly as heavy.

INGREDIENTS

1 head cauliflower, cut into bite-size florets

6 cloves garlic, peeled

1 cup vegetable broth

3 tablespoons unsalted butter

¼ cup minced fresh parsley, plus extra for garnish

Salt and pepper to taste

DIRECTIONS

1. Spray the insert of a 6-quart slow cooker with cooking spray.

2. Place the florets in the slow cooker and top with the garlic cloves, vegetable broth, and enough water to cover the cauliflower, about 4 to 6 cups.

3. Cover and cook for 6 hours on Low or for 3 hours on High. Drain the water and broth and return the cauliflower to the slow cooker. Toss in the butter and use an immersion blender or hand blender to mash.

4. Mix in the parsley, salt, and pepper. Garnish with additional parsley. Keep warm until ready to serve.

Roasted Parmesan Asparagus

My niece hates vegetables. When she comes to visit, I often catch her surreptitiously dropping pieces of broccoli or carrots on the floor for my dog to gobble up. In order to win her over, I sprinkled a bit of cheese on top of the asparagus and told her they were a new version of cheesy fries, and somehow, it worked!

INGREDIENTS

1 bunch asparagus, trimmed

2 tablespoons olive oil

Salt and pepper to taste

¼ cup shredded Parmesan cheese

DIRECTIONS

1. Preheat the oven to 400°F.

2. Lay the asparagus in a single layer on a baking sheet. Drizzle with the olive oil and sprinkle with salt and pepper.

3. Place in the oven and roast until cooked, about 10 minutes.

4. Remove the baking sheet from the oven and sprinkle with the Parmesan cheese.

5. Serve immediately.

NOTES

Baking times will vary greatly due to the size
the parsnips were trimmed to, the moisture content in them, how
thickly the cornstarch was applied, how much oil is used, and
personal taste preferences. They will be prone to burning in the final
minutes of cooking, so keep a watchful
eye as this is a very hot oven.

Baked Parsnip Fries

Yield: Serves 4 | Prep Time: 10 minutes | Cook Time: 35 minutes

Parsnips are a root vegetable, similar to carrots. When I first brought them home, my husband thought I had made some sort of mistake when I was at the farmer's market. The high level of potassium makes them a heart-healthy option and certainly a better alternative to a greasier potato version.

INGREDIENTS

Parsnip Fries

2 pounds parsnips, peeled and trimmed into fries about 5 inches long

2 tablespoons cornstarch

4 tablespoons olive oil

Salt and pepper to taste

Creamy Balsamic Reduction Dip

½ cup balsamic vinegar

3 tablespoons packed light brown sugar

¾ cup sour cream

Scallions, sliced, for garnish

DIRECTIONS

1. *For the parsnip fries:* Preheat the oven to 425°F. Line two baking sheets with parchment paper and set aside.

2. Place the parsnips in a large mixing bowl and sprinkle with the cornstarch. Toss to coat completely. Spread the parsnips onto the baking sheets.

3. Drizzle about 1 tablespoon of the olive oil over each tray and toss the parsnips with your hands to coat. Sprinkle with salt and pepper.

4. Bake on the first side for 20 minutes. Remove the baking sheets from the oven, flip the parsnips over with tongs, drizzle another tablespoon of oil over each tray, and bake for an additional 15 minutes, or until the parsnips are browned and crispy. Remove from the oven and serve immediately.

5. *For the creamy balsamic reduction dip:* While the parsnips are baking, combine the balsamic vinegar and brown sugar in a small saucepan and heat over medium to medium-high heat, stirring constantly until the sugar dissolves. Allow the mixture to come to a boil for 3 minutes, stirring intermittently while it boils.

6. Immediately transfer the reduction to a heat-safe container or bowl and do not let it cool.

7. Combine about 2 tablespoons of the balsamic reduction with the sour cream, to taste, playing with the ratios as desired.

8. Serve the parsnip fries with the sauce and garnish with scallions.

Zucchini Tots

Yield: 12 mini tots | Prep Time: 10 minutes | Cook Time: 18 minutes

Zucchini might just be the most versatile veggie of the bunch. It's a fitting alternative to chicken in the Baked Zucchini Parmesan Casserole (page 155) and even replaced lasagna noodles in the Zucchini Lasagna (page 111). It plays a new role in this recipe by taking the place of potatoes with these fun 'n' friendly tots!

INGREDIENTS

1 zucchini

1 large egg

¼ onion, diced

¼ cup grated reduced-fat sharp cheddar cheese

¼ cup dry Italian bread crumbs

Salt and pepper to taste

Ranch dressing, for serving

DIRECTIONS

1. Preheat the oven to 400°F. Lightly coat a mini muffin tin with cooking spray.

2. Grate the zucchini into a clean dishtowel. Wring as much of the excess water out of the zucchini as you can.

3. In a medium bowl, combine the zucchini, egg, onion, cheddar cheese, bread crumbs, salt, and pepper.

4. Fill each muffin section to the top, pushing down on the filling with your spoon.

5. Bake for 15 to 18 minutes until the tops turn golden.

6. Run a plastic knife around the edges of each tot and pop them out.

7. Serve with ranch dressing or other dip of your choice.

Healthier Green Bean Casserole

Yield: Serves 6 | Prep Time: 25 minutes | Cook Time: 25 minutes

Green bean casseroles come around regularly, whether for a neighborhood potluck or for the holiday season. This recipe has a custom onion topping instead of a store-bought one!

INGREDIENTS

2 pounds fresh green beans, trimmed and cut into bite-size pieces

Mushroom Sauce

2 tablespoons unsalted butter or olive oil

16 ounces white button mushrooms, thinly sliced

4 cloves garlic, minced

3 tablespoons all-purpose flour (or cornstarch, if gluten-free)

½ cup chicken or vegetable stock

½ cup grated Parmesan cheese (not packed)

½ teaspoon kosher salt

¼ teaspoon freshly ground black pepper

Crispy Onion Topping

1 tablespoon unsalted butter or olive oil

1 red onion, thinly sliced

1 cup panko bread crumbs (or gluten-free panko bread crumbs, if gluten-free)

¼ cup freshly grated Parmesan cheese

¼ teaspoon kosher salt

DIRECTIONS

1. Preheat the oven to 375°F. Bring a large stockpot of water to a boil. Add the green beans and boil for 3 to 5 minutes or until crisp-tender. Drain the green beans and set aside.

2. *For the mushroom sauce:* In a large oven-safe skillet, heat the butter over medium-high heat until melted. Add the mushrooms and sauté for 3 to 5 minutes until they are soft and cooked, stirring occasionally. Add the garlic and sauté for an additional 1 to 2 minutes until fragrant, stirring occasionally. Sprinkle with flour and stir to combine. Sauté for an additional minute to cook the flour, stirring occasionally.

3. Slowly add the chicken broth, whisking to combine until smooth. Let cook for an additional minute until thickened, then stir in the Parmesan cheese, salt, and pepper until the cheese is melted. Add the green beans.

4. *For the crispy onion topping:* Heat ½ tablespoon of the butter in a large sauté pan over medium-high heat until melted. Add the onion and sauté, stirring occasionally, for about 5 minutes or until the onion is soft and starting to brown around the edges. Use a slotted spoon to transfer the onion to a separate mixing bowl.

5. Add the remaining ½ tablespoon butter to the pan and melt. Add in the panko and stir until combined. Cook, stirring once every 30 seconds or so, for 3 to 5 minutes until the panko is toasted and lightly golden. Remove from the heat and transfer the panko to the bowl with the onion. Stir in the Parmesan and salt and toss the mixture until combined.

6. Sprinkle the onion topping evenly over the beans. Bake for 25 minutes. Serve.

Spaghetti Squash Casserole

Yield: Serves 6 | Prep Time: 5 minutes | Cook Time: 35 minutes

This dish is versatile because it doubles as both a side dish and a main course. I like to make this at the beginning of the week and dole out portions to serve on the side over the next few days, though you could easily serve this to a family of six as the star attraction!

INGREDIENTS

3 cups cooked spaghetti squash (see Notes)

¾ cup shredded reduced-fat mozzarella cheese

½ cup reduced-fat sour cream

1 large egg, lightly beaten

4 cloves garlic, minced

½ teaspoon kosher salt

¼ teaspoon freshly ground black pepper

¼ teaspoon dried oregano

¼ teaspoon dried thyme

Sour cream, for garnish

Chopped fresh parsley, for garnish

DIRECTIONS

1. Preheat the oven to 400°F. Lightly coat a 9 × 5-inch loaf pan with cooking spray.

2. In a large bowl, combine the spaghetti squash, mozzarella cheese, sour cream, egg, garlic, salt, pepper, oregano, and thyme and place the mixture in the baking dish.

3. Bake for 35 to 40 minutes, or until browned on top and heated through. Garnish with the sour cream and parsley. Scoop and serve.

NOTES

To cook spaghetti squash, slice it in half lengthwise. Drizzle with olive oil and place on a baking sheet. Bake at 400°F until tender, approximately 20 minutes.

One 2½-pound spaghetti squash will yield about 3 cups.

Lighter Corn Casserole

Yield: Serves 10 | Prep Time: 10 minutes | Cook Time: 35–40 minutes

In this recipe, Greek yogurt replaces some of the high-fat ingredients like sour cream or butter that usually dominate a corn casserole. That way you get all of the tastiness of a creamy favorite without all the unhealthy drawbacks.

INGREDIENTS

1 large egg

1 egg white

1 cup plain Greek yogurt

3 tablespoons unsalted butter, melted

1 (15.25-ounce) can whole kernel corn, drained

1 (14.75-ounce) can cream-style golden sweet corn

1 (8.5-ounce) package corn muffin mix

DIRECTIONS

1. Preheat the oven to 350°F. Lightly coat an 8 × 8-inch baking dish with cooking spray.

2. In large mixing bowl, whisk together the egg and egg white. Stir in the Greek yogurt and melted butter.

3. Stir in the whole kernel corn, golden sweet corn, and corn muffin mix.

4. Pour into the baking dish and bake for 35 to 40 minutes or until the center is set and the top is lightly golden brown. Slice and serve.

Butternut Squash Home Fries

Yield: Serves 4 | Prep Time: 10 minutes | Cook Time: 40 minutes

Sometimes I'll snack on these instead of potato fries while I'm catching up on my favorite TV shows. Crispy on the outside and smooth on the inside, these fries are a simple yet effective way to curb any pangs of hunger. And since they're baked instead of fried, they aren't loaded down with unnecessary fats and oils.

INGREDIENTS

1 butternut squash, peeled and cut into ½-inch cubes

2 tablespoons olive oil

Salt and pepper to taste

Ketchup, for serving

DIRECTIONS

1. Preheat the oven to 400°F. Line a baking sheet with parchment paper.

2. Place the squash on the baking sheet and drizzle with the olive oil. Add salt and pepper and toss to coat so that all of the squash cubes are evenly coated.

3. Bake for 35 to 40 minutes or until golden brown to your liking. Toss every 10 minutes.

4. Serve warm with ketchup.

Roasted Sweet Potatoes and Brussels Sprouts

Yield: Serves 6–8 | Prep Time: 15 minutes | Cook Time: 45 minutes

The first time I combined creamy sweet potatoes with crunchier Brussels sprouts, I was in love. Sometimes the most unexpected combinations are the best ones. Sweet potatoes are an excellent source of vitamin A, while Brussels sprouts are rich in vitamins C and K. You're practically getting the whole alphabet involved in a single dish!

INGREDIENTS

1 pound Brussels sprouts, trimmed and halved

2 large sweet potatoes, cut into 1-inch cubes

4 cloves garlic, smashed

⅓ cup olive oil, plus extra for the pan

¼ teaspoon garlic salt

Salt and pepper to taste

1–2 tablespoons red wine vinegar

DIRECTIONS

1. Preheat the oven to 400°F.

2. Place the Brussels sprouts, sweet potatoes, and garlic in a large bowl.

3. Pour the olive oil over the vegetables.

4. Add the garlic salt, and salt and pepper to taste. Stir to coat.

5. Drizzle a little olive oil onto the baking sheet and spread evenly with a brush.

6. Pour the veggies onto the pan.

7. Roast for 40 to 45 minutes. The veggies are done when they are brown and a fork slides into them easily.

8. Place the veggies in a serving bowl and toss with the red wine vinegar to taste. Serve.

Garlic Mushroom Quinoa with Brussels Sprouts

Yield: Serves 6 | Prep Time: 10 minutes | Cook Time: 25 minutes

Replacing rice with quinoa can make a huge difference in terms of nutrition. It's higher in potassium, protein, calcium, iron, and much more, making it a food that ought to be a staple in everyone's diet. The sharp garlic flavor gives this dish plenty of personality.

INGREDIENTS

1 cup uncooked quinoa

1 pound Brussels sprouts

1 tablespoon olive oil

1 pound cremini mushrooms, thinly sliced

4 cloves garlic, minced

½ teaspoon dried thyme

Salt and pepper

2 tablespoons grated Parmesan cheese

Fresh thyme, for garnish

DIRECTIONS

1. In a large saucepan, cook the quinoa according to the package instructions. Pour into a large bowl and set aside.

2. In a large saucepan, blanch the Brussels sprouts in 2 cups salted water over medium-high heat for 5 minutes. Remove from the water and set aside.

3. Heat the olive oil in a large skillet over medium-high heat. Add the mushrooms, garlic, and dried thyme, and cook, stirring occasionally, for 3 to 4 minutes until tender. Season with salt and pepper to taste. Stir the mushrooms and Brussels sprouts into the quinoa until well combined.

4. Serve immediately, topped with the Parmesan cheese and fresh thyme.

Pac-Man Potatoes

Yield: Serves 2–4 | Prep Time: 5 minutes | Cook Time: 30 minutes

How fun are these potatoes? I like to call them Pac-Man potatoes because the gaps on the side used for venting remind me of the mouth I would see gobbling up those little white dots. This was one of my winning dishes on *Food Network Star*!

INGREDIENTS

1 pound baby red potatoes

2 tablespoons olive oil

Salt and pepper to taste

1 cup ranch dressing

¼ cup sriracha sauce

DIRECTIONS

1. Preheat the oven to 400°F.

2. Place the potatoes on a baking sheet, drizzle with olive oil, and season with salt and pepper.

3. Bake for 20 to 30 minutes until the potatoes are tender and cooked through.

4. Remove from the oven and lightly smash with a meat mallet. They will burst slightly, forming a shape that resembles the mouth of a Pac-Man character.

5. Return to the oven and bake for an additional 10 to 20 minutes until golden brown and crispy.

6. In a small bowl, combine the ranch dressing and sriracha sauce for dipping. Season with salt and pepper.

7. Serve the potatoes with the dipping sauce.

7

Dessert

You can still indulge in dessert even if you're trying to eat healthier; you just need to have a strategy going in. Avoid the fudgy chocolate and aim for lighter, fruitier dishes like Blueberry Frozen Yogurt (page 194) or Tropical Breeze Dessert (page 197). Find lightened-up versions of country-style favorites like Apple Pie Oatmeal Cookies (page 206) or Peanut Butter Banana Cookies (page 209). The trick to healthy dessert isn't complete deprivation, it's just finding ways to make your favorite foods a little more wholesome.

24-Hour Fruit Salad

Yield: Serves 8 | Prep Time: 15 minutes | Cook Time: N/A

Dessert can be one of the most difficult things to give up when you're trying to eat healthier. As I sadly turn away offers of pies, cakes, and more, I happily turn toward this fruit salad recipe, which has enough fruity toppings to remind me of fro-yo while helping me stick to my healthy-eating resolution.

INGREDIENTS

2 cups Greek yogurt, plain or vanilla

1 orange, zested, peeled, and cut into bite-size pieces

2 cups pineapple chunks, fresh or canned

2 cups fresh or frozen berries

1 cup diced fresh or frozen peaches

1 cup green or red grapes, cut in half

¼ cup coconut flakes, sweetened or unsweetened, toasted

Fresh mint sprigs, for garnish

DIRECTIONS

1. In a large bowl, combine the yogurt and orange zest.

2. Add the orange pieces, pineapple, berries, peaches, and grapes. Stir to combine.

3. The salad can be served right away or chilled for up to 24 hours. Sprinkle the top with the coconut and add a sprig of fresh mint before serving.

NOTES

To toast the coconut, cook at 350°F on a baking sheet for 5 to 10 minutes.

Blueberry Frozen Yogurt

Yield: Serves 4 | Prep Time: 5 minutes | Chill Time: 1 hour

Homemade frozen yogurt is so much easier to make than you might think. When I tell people that I make my own, they ask me whether I had to buy an expensive ice cream machine or purchase dry ice, and I just tell them that all they need is a blender and a freezer!

INGREDIENTS

4 cups frozen blueberries

½ cup nonfat coconut-flavored yogurt

3 tablespoons honey

1 tablespoon lime juice

¼ teaspoon coconut extract

Chopped pistachios, for garnish

DIRECTIONS

1. Combine the blueberries, yogurt, honey, lime juice, and coconut extract in a blender.

2. Blend for 5 minutes until smooth.

3. Chill in the freezer until set, about 1 hour.

4. Garnish with chopped pistachios. Serve.

Tropical Breeze Dessert

Yield: Serves 8 | Prep Time: 5 minutes | Chill Time: 1–2 hours

I can eat more than my fair share of this Tropical Breeze Dessert without feeling like I need to lie down afterward. It's a palate cleanser that works wonderfully at the end of a big meal.

INGREDIENTS

1 (15-ounce) can crushed pineapple in juice

1 (1-ounce) package sugar-free instant vanilla pudding mix

1 (12-ounce) container reduced-fat whipped topping, thawed

1 cup mini marshmallows

½ teaspoon rum extract

Sweetened shredded coconut, toasted, for garnish

DIRECTIONS

1. In a medium bowl, combine the pineapple with its juice and the pudding mix.

2. Gradually fold in the whipped topping.

3. Stir in the marshmallows and rum extract.

4. Place the mixture into eight dessert dishes or glasses.

5. Chill for 1 to 2 hours until set.

6. Garnish with toasted coconut and serve.

NOTES

To toast the coconut, cook at 350°F on a baking sheet for 5 to 10 minutes.

Avocado Chocolate Pudding

Yield: Serves 3 | Prep Time: 5 minutes | Cook Time: N/A

Homemade chocolate pudding removes many of the artificial preservatives that the store-bought version often has. What makes this recipe unique has to be the avocados. They provide the smooth creaminess for the pudding in a nutritious way. The maple syrup adds the sweetness the dish needs without the artificial quality of added sugar while the coconut milk is a lighter alternative to the typical heavy cream.

INGREDIENTS

2 ripe avocados, peeled and chopped

⅓ cup unsweetened cocoa powder

½ cup coconut milk or almond milk

¼ cup maple syrup

1½ teaspoons vanilla extract

¼ teaspoon instant espresso powder

DIRECTIONS

1. Blend the avocados, cocoa powder, coconut milk, maple syrup, vanilla, and espresso powder until smooth in a food processor or in a bowl using a handheld mixer.

2. Spoon into dessert cups.

3. Serve immediately or chill.

Slow Cooker Peach Cobbler

Yield: Serves 6 | Prep Time: 10 minutes | Cook Time: 4–5 hours on Low

Peaches, oats, and cinnamon are an irresistible combination. The oats, rich in antioxidants, are a much more nutritious counter to the peaches than the dough in a more traditional version.

INGREDIENTS

4 cups sliced peaches, fresh or canned

⅔ cup quick-cooking oats

½ cup packed light brown sugar

⅓ cup buttermilk baking mix

½ teaspoon cinnamon

½ teaspoon nutmeg

¼ teaspoon almond extract

¼ teaspoon kosher salt

½ cup peach juice or nectar

2 tablespoons peach jam

Vanilla frozen yogurt or ice cream, for serving

DIRECTIONS

1. Spray the insert of a 6-quart slow cooker with cooking spray.

2. Place the peaches in the slow cooker.

3. In a large bowl, combine the oats, brown sugar, buttermilk baking mix, cinnamon, nutmeg, almond extract, and salt. Pour over the peaches.

4. Mix the peach juice with the peach jam and pour over the baking mixture. Gently stir to combine.

5. Place some paper towels under the cover to help with condensation. Cover and cook for 4 to 5 hours on Low.

6. Serve with vanilla frozen yogurt or ice cream.

Gluten-Free Chocolate Brownies

Yield: 16 brownies │ Prep Time: 15 minutes │ Cook Time: 35–45 minutes

Gluten can cause digestive issues (or worse) for many, so I try to go gluten-free any time I'm baking for a large crowd. The best part about this recipe is that I can serve it to my non-gluten-free friends, and they can't tell the difference because all they can taste is the delicious combination of dark chocolate and espresso powder.

INGREDIENTS

⅓ cup almond flour

⅓ cup coconut flour

1 tablespoon unsweetened cocoa powder

1 teaspoon espresso powder

½ teaspoon kosher salt

6 ounces dark chocolate, chopped

½ cup coconut oil

1 cup organic sugar

2 large eggs

1 teaspoon vanilla extract

1 cup bittersweet dark chocolate chips

DIRECTIONS

1. Preheat the oven to 350°F. Line an 8 × 8-inch baking dish with parchment paper, leaving an overhang. Lightly coat the parchment paper with cooking spray.

2. In a medium bowl, whisk together the almond flour, coconut flour, cocoa powder, espresso powder, and salt.

3. Place the chopped dark chocolate and coconut oil in a large bowl. Microwave for 30 seconds, stir, and repeat until the chocolate and coconut oil are melted.

4. Mix in the sugar until combined. Let cool.

5. Add the eggs to the cooled chocolate mixture and stir in the vanilla.

6. Fold in the flour mixture, then the chocolate chips. Spread the batter in the baking pan.

7. Bake for 35 to 45 minutes until a toothpick inserted into the center comes out with moist crumbs.

8. Cool in the pan for 15 minutes, then carefully lift the brownies by the parchment paper and set on a wire rack to cool completely. Cut into 16 squares and serve.

Strawberry Oatmeal Bars

Yield: 12 bars | Prep Time: 10 minutes | Cook Time: 45–50 minutes

Oats are chock-full of fiber and minerals, which make them ideal combatants against heart disease and diabetes. I've added a sweeter component with some juicy strawberries to make these oatmeal bars shiny and new. Plus, I can make a batch for dessert and continue to snack on them for breakfast the next morning!

INGREDIENTS

2 cups strawberries, diced small

1 tablespoon granulated sugar

1 tablespoon fresh lemon juice

1 cup old-fashioned rolled oats

¾ cup all-purpose flour

⅓ cup packed dark brown sugar

¼ teaspoon ground ginger

¼ teaspoon kosher salt

6 tablespoons unsalted butter, melted

1 teaspoon cornstarch

DIRECTIONS

1. Preheat the oven to 375°F. Line an 8 × 8-inch baking pan with parchment paper.

2. In a medium bowl, combine the strawberries, granulated sugar, and lemon juice. Set aside and allow to macerate while preparing the remaining ingredients.

3. In another medium bowl, combine the oats, flour, brown sugar, ginger, and salt. Pour in the melted butter and stir until everything is well combined. The mixture will be crumbly and loose. Measure out ½ cup of the crumble mixture and set aside. Carefully press the remaining mixture into an even layer in the bottom of the prepared baking dish.

4. Scatter the strawberry mixture over the crust. Lightly sprinkle cornstarch over the top of the strawberries, followed by the reserved crumbs.

5. Bake the bars for 45 to 50 minutes until the bottom is firm and the topping is golden brown.

6. Remove from the oven and cool completely before cutting.

7. Cut into 12 bars and serve.

Apple Pie Oatmeal Cookies

Yield: 15 cookies | Prep Time: 10 minutes plus 30 minutes chill time | Cook Time: 12–15 minutes

It may seem very all-American of me, but there's no pie I enjoy more than a home-cooked apple pie. I go apple picking with my friends every fall, and I often end up baking at least four pies with my haul. I challenged myself to find a healthier version and came up with this handy oatmeal cookie variation. The portion sizes are smaller, and the oats add a nutritious boost!

INGREDIENTS

Cookies

1 cup instant oats

¾ cup whole-wheat flour

1½ teaspoons baking powder

1 teaspoon cinnamon

½ teaspoon cardamom

⅛ teaspoon kosher salt

2 tablespoons unsalted butter, melted

1 large egg, room temperature

1 teaspoon vanilla extract

¼ cup agave

¼ cup maple syrup

1 cup finely diced peeled red apple

Glaze

1 cup confectioners' sugar

3 tablespoons maple syrup

DIRECTIONS

1. *For the cookies:* In a medium bowl, mix together the oats, flour, baking powder, cinnamon, cardamom, and salt.

2. In another medium bowl, whisk the melted butter, egg, and vanilla. Add in the agave and maple syrup.

3. Add the flour mixture to the egg mixture, then add the diced apples. Stir. Chill for 30 minutes.

4. Preheat the oven to 350°F. Line a baking sheet with parchment paper.

5. Scoop the cookie dough onto the baking sheet in 2-tablespoon portions. Flatten the cookies with the back of a spoon.

6. Bake for 12 to 15 minutes or until lightly browned.

7. Cool on the baking sheet for 10 minutes. Place the cookies on a wire rack to cool completely.

8. *For the glaze:* Whisk the confectioners' sugar with the maple syrup to a consistency for a drizzle.

9. Drizzle the glaze over the cookies and serve.

Peanut Butter Banana Cookies

Yield: 18 cookies | Prep Time: 15 minutes | Cook Time: 10–15 minutes

Elvis was known for not only his rock 'n' roll hits, but also his penchant for peanut butter and banana foods. I know he would've loved these cookies, which combine the two flavors (along with a hint of chocolate and cinnamon) into a gluten-free cookie that's too good to pass up! Truvia is a calorie-free alternative to sugar.

INGREDIENTS

1 ripe banana

⅓ cup coconut flour

¼ cup mini chocolate chips

2 tablespoons creamy peanut butter

½ teaspoon vanilla extract

½ teaspoon Truvia

¼ teaspoon cinnamon

DIRECTIONS

1. Preheat the oven to 350°F. Line a baking sheet with parchment paper.

2. Place the banana in a medium bowl and mash it. Mix in the coconut flour, chocolate chips, peanut butter, vanilla, Truvia, and cinnamon.

3. Form the dough into ½-inch balls and place on the baking sheet, flattening the cookies with a fork to make crisscross marks.

4. Bake for 10 to 15 minutes until the cookies are golden.

5. Let cool on the pan for 10 minutes, then place on a wire rack to cool completely. Serve.

Lightened-Up Pumpkin Pie in a Mug

Yield: 1 cake | Prep Time: 5 minutes | Cook Time: 2 minutes

While my favorite pie flavor has always been apple, my husband prefers pumpkin. (It can get a little tense in our house once fall rolls around!) By using coconut milk and pumpkin pie spice, you can maintain the sweetness of the dish while making it more nutritious.

INGREDIENTS

¼ cup whole-wheat flour

2 tablespoons pumpkin puree

2 tablespoons sugar

2 tablespoons coconut milk

½ tablespoon vegetable oil

¼ teaspoon baking powder

⅛ teaspoon cinnamon

⅛ teaspoon pumpkin pie spice

Pinch of salt

DIRECTIONS

1. In an 8-ounce microwave-safe mug, combine all of the ingredients. Mix with a small whisk until the batter is smooth.

2. Cook in the microwave for 1 minute 45 seconds on high. Add 15 seconds at a time if needed. Serve immediately.

Greek Yogurt Cake

Yield: Serves 10 | Prep Time: 10 minutes | Cook Time: 35–40 minutes

The Greek yogurt in this recipe makes the cake extra moist, so your fork gracefully slides through as you take each bite. I topped it with confectioners' sugar and slices of strawberry, but it's easy to customize it how you like, whether you add cinnamon sugar, mixed berries, or even a chocolate drizzle.

INGREDIENTS

3 large eggs

1 cup granulated sugar

1 cup vanilla or honey Greek yogurt (or use the flavor you like)

½ cup vegetable oil

1 tablespoon orange zest

½ teaspoon almond extract

1½ cups all-purpose flour

1 tablespoon baking powder

¼ teaspoon kosher salt

Confectioners' sugar, for dusting

Sliced strawberries, for garnish

DIRECTIONS

1. Preheat the oven to 350°F. Lightly coat a 9-inch springform pan with cooking spray.

2. In a medium bowl, beat the eggs with a hand mixer on medium speed for 1 minute.

3. Add the granulated sugar, yogurt, and oil and mix for 1 minute. Add the orange zest and almond extract.

4. Next add the flour, baking powder, and salt and beat until incorporated.

5. Pour the batter into the pan and bake for 35 to 40 minutes until a toothpick inserted into the middle of the cake comes out clean.

6. Remove the cake and place on a wire rack for 5 minutes.

7. When the cake is cool, sprinkle with confectioners' sugar and top with sliced strawberries. Cut into slices and serve.

Chocolate Lover's Zucchini Cake

Yield: Serves 10–12 | Prep Time: 35 minutes | Cook Time: 45 minutes

Once again, it's zucchini to the rescue! If you simply must indulge in chocolate, this is the dessert I recommend. Zucchini contains quite a bit of potassium, which helps reduce blood pressure, so really, eating this cake is a calming practice.

INGREDIENTS

Cake

2½ cups all-purpose flour, plus extra for dusting the pan

½ cup unsweetened cocoa powder, plus extra for dusting the pan

2 cups sugar

¾ cup vegetable oil

3 large eggs

2 teaspoons vanilla extract

1½ teaspoons baking powder

1½ teaspoons baking soda

1 teaspoon instant espresso powder

1 teaspoon cinnamon

½ teaspoon kosher salt

½ cup low-fat buttermilk

2¼ cups shredded zucchini

2 teaspoons orange zest

Glaze

1 cup confectioners' sugar

1½ tablespoons 2% milk

½ teaspoon vanilla extract

DIRECTIONS

1. *For the cake:* Preheat the oven to 325°F. Grease the inside of a Bundt pan with cooking spray or butter and sprinkle a bit of flour and cocoa to coat. Shake out any excess flour and cocoa.

2. In a large bowl, combine the sugar, oil, and eggs until mixed. Add the vanilla.

3. In a small bowl, whisk together the flour, cocoa powder, baking powder, baking soda, espresso powder, cinnamon, and salt.

4. Add the flour mixture to the sugar mixture. Stir until well combined.

5. Stir in the buttermilk, then add in the zucchini and orange zest.

6. Pour the batter into the Bundt pan.

7. Bake for 45 to 55 minutes or until a toothpick inserted into the center comes out clean.

8. Cool the cake in the pan for 15 to 20 minutes. Carefully invert the cake on a wire rack to cool completely.

9. *For the glaze:* Combine the confectioners' sugar, milk, and vanilla until you have a pourable consistency to drizzle over the cake. Allow it to set for about 5 minutes before slicing and serving.

Clean-Eating Carrot Cake

Yield: Serves 9 | Prep Time: 20 minutes | Cook Time: 28–32 minutes

My cousin goes through a health-conscious spring cleaning every year, which limits what he can eat at the Easter table. Last year, I showed up with this carrot cake and told him how the coconut oil, whole-wheat flour, and Greek yogurt help keep this carrot cake recipe nutritious. He was so pleased, and for the first time in years, he actually allowed himself to enjoy some dessert.

INGREDIENTS

Cake

1½ cups whole-wheat flour

1½ teaspoons baking powder

1½ teaspoons cinnamon

½ teaspoon baking soda

½ teaspoon nutmeg

¼ teaspoon kosher salt

1 tablespoon coconut oil, melted and cooled

1 large egg

2 teaspoons vanilla extract

½ cup maple syrup

¼ cup plain Greek yogurt

¼ cup 1% milk

2 cups grated carrots

½ cup raisins

¼ cup chopped walnuts

2 tablespoons chopped dried pineapple

Frosting

8 ounces reduced-fat cream cheese

1 cup confectioners' sugar

2 tablespoons coconut yogurt

1 teaspoon vanilla extract

Chopped walnuts, for garnish

DIRECTIONS

1. *For the cake:* Preheat the oven to 350°F. Lightly coat a 9 × 9-inch baking pan with cooking spray.

2. In a large bowl, whisk together the flour, baking powder, cinnamon, baking soda, nutmeg, and salt.

3. In a small bowl, combine the coconut oil, egg, and vanilla. Next mix in the maple syrup and yogurt.

4. Alternate combining the milk and the yogurt mixture into the flour bowl until well combined.

5. Add the carrots, raisins, walnuts, and pineapple.

6. Spread the batter in the baking pan. Bake for 28 to 32 minutes until a toothpick inserted into the center comes out clean.

7. Cool in the pan for 10 to 15 minutes. Place on a wire rack to cool completely.

8. *For the frosting:* In a medium bowl, mix together the cream cheese, confectioners' sugar, yogurt, and vanilla.

9. Spread the frosting on the cake and top with the chopped walnuts.

10. Let set for 1 hour at room temperature. Slice and serve.

Banana Cheesecakes

Yield: Serves 2 | Prep Time: 10 minutes plus 2–3 hours chilling time | Cook Time: 30 minutes

The oats and applesauce form a healthy crust which makes these cakes much better for cheesecake lovers everywhere. My favorite part about this dish, however, is the hint of honey used in the filling. It's an extra burst of sugary sweetness that makes it feel like you're treating yourself to something special.

INGREDIENTS

¼ cup quick-cooking oats

2 tablespoons unsweetened applesauce

4 ounces reduced-fat cream cheese

2 ounces low-fat sour cream

1 tablespoon honey

¼ cup mashed ripe banana

½ teaspoon cornstarch

¼ teaspoon almond extract

1 banana, sliced, for garnish

DIRECTIONS

1. Preheat the oven to 300°F. Lightly coat two individual cheesecake molds or two jumbo-sized muffin cups with cooking spray.

2. In a small bowl, combine the oats and applesauce. Divide the mixture and gently press into the bottoms of the molds.

3. Bake for 8 minutes. Leave the oven on as you let the molds cool.

4. In a medium bowl, mix the cream cheese, sour cream, and honey until smooth.

5. Mix in the mashed banana, cornstarch, and almond extract.

6. Spoon the filling over the cooled crusts and bake for 18 to 22 minutes until the cheesecakes are mostly set. They should jiggle a bit.

7. Cool to room temperature, then chill for 2 to 3 hours.

8. Carefully remove from the molds and serve, garnished with banana slices.

Greek Yogurt Fruit Tart

Yield: Serves 8–10 | Prep Time: 25 minutes | Cook Time: N/A

The date, oat, and walnut crust is something I had heard about from a health-conscious friend of mine, and I knew I had to try it out! With just a touch of fruity flavor, it's almost as much of a star as the creamy fruit filling.

INGREDIENTS

16 Medjool dates, pits removed, soaked in warm water for 10–15 minutes

1 cup raw walnuts

½ cup quick-cooking oats

1 cup vanilla Greek yogurt

1 tablespoon honey

½ teaspoon orange zest

½ teaspoon vanilla extract

Assorted sliced fresh fruits

DIRECTIONS

1. Lightly coat a 9-inch tart pan with cooking spray.

2. Drain the dates and then coarsely chop.

3. In a food processor, pulse the dates, walnuts, and oats until a thick dough is formed.

4. Press the dough evenly into the bottom and up the sides of the tart pan.

5. Mix the yogurt with the honey, orange zest, and vanilla.

6. Spread the yogurt over the crust.

7. Decorate with sliced fresh fruit. Serve.

Acknowledgments

As small children, Sarah and I spent time together! My memory is hazy, but I do recall hanging in the Gundrys' old house in Wayzata. I remember going to our cabin, and like any siblings would do, we created a little storefront where we could sell rocks that we found on the beach. We probably made Alex buy them. When Alex and I started dating, Sarah and I started spending more adult time together. We have been able to experience our own incredible milestones together, like getting a puppy, buying a house, engagements, and weddings! Because of Sarah's kindness and warmth, her wit and her spunk, somewhere along the road Sarah went from being my boyfriend's sister to my own. Thank you for being the best sister I could ever ask for.

Thank you to my incredible culinary and creative team at Prime Publishing. Megan Von Schönhoff and Tom Krawczyk, my photographers. Chris Hammond, Judith Hines, and Marlene Stolfo, my culinary test kitchen geniuses. To word masters and editors Bryn Clark and Jessica Thelander. And to my amazing editor and friend, Kara Rota. Thank you to Stuart Hochwert and the entire Prime Publishing team for their enthusiasm and support. Thank you to Will Schwalbe, Erica Martirano, Justine Sha, Jaclyn Waggner, and the entire staff at St. Martin's Griffin, for helping this book come to life. This book was a team effort, filled with collaboration and creativity that reached no limits.

Index

About the Author

After receiving her master's in culinary arts at Auguste Escoffier in Avignon, France, Addie stayed in France to learn from Christian Etienne at his three-Michelin-star restaurant. Upon leaving France, she spent the next several years working with restaurant groups. She worked in the kitchen for Daniel Boulud and moved coast-to-coast with Thomas Keller building a career in management, restaurant openings, and brand development. She later joined Martha Stewart Living Omnimedia, where she worked with the editorial team as well as in marketing and sales. While living in New York, Addie completed her bachelor's degree in organizational behavior. Upon leaving New York, Addie joined gravitytank, an innovation consultancy in Chicago. As a culinary designer at gravitytank, Addie designed new food products for companies, large and small. She created edible prototypes for clients and research participants to taste and experience, some of which you may see in stores today. In 2015, she debuted on the Food Network, where she competed on *Cutthroat Kitchen*, and won! In 2017, she competed on the thirteenth season of *Food Network Star*.

Addie is the executive producer for RecipeLion. Addie oversees and creates culinary content for multiple web platforms and communities, leads video strategy, and oversees the production of in-print books. Addie is passionate about taking easy recipes and making them elegant, without making them complicated. From fine dining to entertain-ing, to innovation and test kitchens, Addie's experience with food makes these recipes unique and delicious.

Addie and her husband live in Lake Forest, Illinois, with their baby boy and happy puppy, Paisley. Addie is actively involved with youth culinary programs in the Chicagoland area, serving on the board of a bakery and catering company that employs at-risk youth. She is a healthy-food teacher for first-graders in a low-income school district, and aside from eating and entertaining with friends and family, she loves encouraging kids to be creative in the kitchen!